2012

To John

My prayer is that God gives
you both Prosperity and Purpose.
I see I beg future for you
stay true to what your heart
tells you.

Enjoy the book!

PROSPERITY

— WITH —

PURPOSE

This is a powerfully moving story, told in stark honesty. I have hoped for some time that Mike would one day write his dramatic story. I have observed the integrity of his faith and character for many years yet I found myself amazed at the quality and depth of this book. If you want to return to a right foundation, if you want to uncomplicate your life, if you want to hear what Jesus is saying to you today, read on.

John Dawson, *President, Youth With A Mission*

"Reading Mike's book and knowing him as a person is like hearing of a man's quest to summit Mt. Everest, and watching him snowboard back to base camp. You are not going to want to put this book down."

Danny Silk, *author of Culture of Honor: Sustaining a Supernatural Environment, founder of Loving on Purpose Educational Services and Global Transformation Institute*

"Prosperity with Purpose not only tells the story of Mike's corporate success, but also his resolute determination to overcome tragedy. It acts as a worthwhile and heartening guide to whichever station of life you may find yourself. Mike is a personal friend and I know that he walks out the truths that he speaks. You will be inspired by this book."

Mike Bickle, *author of several books including Passion for Jesus, Growing in the Prophetic, The Pleasures of Loving God, After God's Own Heart, Prayers to Strengthen Your Inner Man, and the Director of the International House of Prayer Missions Base of Kansas City (IHOP–KC)*

Mike Frank is the real deal. He has known great success. He has experienced great sorrow. The Lord has tenderized his heart. If you want insights on how to keep life priorities and encouragement in making the hard decisions, read this book.

Don Finto, *author of Your People Shall be My People, and Founder & President, Caleb/Joshua Generations*

I've heard Mike Frank tell his story in person four times, and yet reading his book brought details to me in a whole new way that made me feel more human and alive. He shares his life so personally that you feel like you were there with him step by step, seeing what he saw and feeling what he felt at the time. The things that changed Mike have the power to change us all. Mike Frank faced his pain. In facing it, he transcended it because God used it to transform him. This is the story of a man who dared to enter into the drama of his own life, and there he found God, along with his wife and children. Mike's success made him successful, but it was God Who made him rich in love. I hope many people read this. I recommend it highly, especially to men and women who really want their lives to count.

Sarah Sumner, *author of Leadership Above the Line*

MIKE FRANK

PROSPERITY
— WITH —
PURPOSE

An Executive's Search for Significance

SLINGSTONE
MEDIA

PROSPERITY WITH PURPOSE:
AN EXECUTIVE'S SEARCH FOR SIGNIFICANCE
Copyright © 2011 by Mike Frank

SLINGSTONE
MEDIA

Slingstone Media, LLC
Redding, California

Scripture taken from the New King James Version of the Bible.
Copyright © 1982 by Thomas Nelson, Inc. Used by permission. All
rights reserved.

FIRST EDITION

Author Photograph © Mike Skilleter
Book cover design by Samuel Nudds
Layout design by Renee Evans and Layla Smith

ISBN 978-0-9838140-0-9
Library of Congress Control Number: 2011934020

Printed in the United States of America
www.slingstonemedia.com

TO LEXIE

who taught me how to love

CONTENTS

— Author's Note —

NOT LONG AGO I sat in a coaching meeting while overlooking the ocean in Santa Barbara, the most luxurious city in California. Palm trees and European cafés line the walkways that lead to a quaint wharf, idyllic harbor, lengthy beaches and lapping waves. It is utterly pristine.

"To be honest, Mike," my client said, his impatience becoming evident, "all I want to know is how you became successful."

He had been an executive vice president at a respected college in southern California, had prospered financially, was happily married and had a seemingly healthy family. From the outside, he had *already* been successful, not only in occupation, but in life. He lived the American Dream.

Yet here he was in his 50's, still looking for a magic formula for what he referred to as "success." What was he missing? Some describe it as a gnawing, empty feeling of something unknown, something unexplainable.

Is this all there is? There has to be more…

After years of doing what he thought would bring him happiness, questions glared at him, demanding answers. He had none.

My answer?

He simply needed someone to give him permission to be a man outside of his job. Metaphorically speaking, my client needed to be given permission to go on the most significant journey of his life— to slay dragons, save a damsel in distress and send a rock spiraling through the air to knock down Goliath! How is that different than what he had already accomplished? It's a matter of perspective. He wasn't living an adventure, and the only way he could change that fact was to lend purpose to his prosperity.

Like many people, my client failed to realize that there is no success without significance, and wealth is a byproduct, not a goal. Hundreds of books have been written on wealth, but none of them contain the "Holy Grail" that answers the myriad of questions on the subject. They might have a modicum of breakthrough, or a few tactics and tips, but that is all. Most people want a step-by-step guide toward corporate success, but in good conscience, I must dispel this misplaced trust. There isn't a formula for success, significance or wealth.

There have been several impossible situations in my life that I would not wish upon my worst enemy. However, through these events, I have gained perspective that has enabled me to provide hope, comfort, and depth of experience. Within this book, I have included several life lessons that will hopefully assist you in your journey towards genuine success through legitimate significance, which may or may not include unfathomable wealth. But I should remind you that this is merely one man's journey. That being said, welcome to the story of my life…

CHAPTER 1

— Piercing the Cold Heart —

"Now I know I've got a heart,
'cause it's breaking…"
THE WIZARD OF OZ [2]

A YOUNG GIRL stood out from the crowd as we walked by huddled groups of women in the refugee camp. Her skin glistened with sweat and the distinctive red dirt of Africa. She was too young to be a mother, yet a tiny baby was nestled in her arms. Her desperation was evident, and I felt my heart surge with emotion.

The women distrusted us, a group of light-skinned male "rescuers" with World Relief. Some were even terrified. The men they had previously known raped their bodies, ravaging their self-worth. They wore ragged and faded clothes with gaping holes. I could see misery in their eyes. Hopelessness. Most of them were hollow beings, overcome by trauma. Their sanity teetered on the edge of insanity.

I was only just beginning to understand brokenness like theirs. Three years before I had been introduced to my life's first tragic situation, and I still didn't know if I would have the strength to recover. But now, by witnessing the sorrow that consumed these women, I was able to see a deeper perspective of my life—I was being ruined by compassion, and I was grateful.

It was time to leave. As I climbed up into the seat of my team's Land Rover, I noticed that the girl with the dark shiny skin had followed me. She ran up to the open door and shoved her little girl into my arms. I responded intuitively, cradling her small child before I realized what I had done. My arms ached for the weight of my two year old back home in Omaha, Nebraska. My baby girl, the one who I believed must have been sent to me for a divine purpose. Her birth had initiated my heart's greatest journey.

Using broken English phrases, the girl spoke forcefully, "You take her. I want you to have her. If she stays here, she dies!"

The year was 2000. Our World Relief team had traveled the dusty roads of Sierra Leone with the goal of bringing food and encouragement to the inhabitants of a war-torn nation. The girl that stood in front of me was a former sex slave of the rebel RUF soldiers.

Once again my heart was jolted at the sight of her desolation. I could not refuse her. What I could not do for my own baby back home, I wanted to do for this girl's child. Yet I knew that legally, I could do nothing. Nor was my studied and analytical expertise as a business executive helpful in knowing how to respond to her personal tragedy.

Oh God, I thought. *How can I leave her this way?*

The girl's forcefulness, turned into screaming, "You take her!"

My tongue felt immobile. Finally, I said painfully, "I can't! There's no way I could smuggle her out of the country."

She chose not to hear my words. "I can't keep her here! You must take her!"

I began to weep.

The girl turned and walked away without looking back.

I sat transfixed, emotionally torn and unable to take action.

"COUNT ME IN"

Clive Calver, the president of World Relief, had asked me to join him on this ten-day trip to Sierra Leone, which occupied the western hemisphere of one of the most fabled continents in history—Africa. British, armed with a PhD in Theology and a compassionate heart, Clive was fearless. Civil war, famine, and highly precarious situations never deterred him.

At the time, I was two years out of a company, Level 3 Communications, which was the darling of Wall Street. The company was flying high. I used to be one of their top men, running strong in the marketplace, competing to win, making a difference and being someone with power, influence and momentum. I hadn't wished to leave. In fact, I had clung to Level 3 as long as I could. But my family had been faced with multiple heart-breaking circumstances that required all of me. It was one of the toughest decisions I had ever made. I knew that leaving my corporate job to care for my family had been the right decision, but there was still a part of me that dreamt of soaring with Level 3 in the corporate world. I was floundering, not knowing who I was without my persona of "highly successful, money-making, head-turning senior executive" who was on the envious list of nation-wide headhunters.

I had obsessed about the scoreboard my entire life, thinking, *How am I going to get higher in the 'pecking order'?*

Now I was challenged with questions I had never asked before:

Who am I?

What is my purpose?

And most frightening of all, *Where am I going?*

As a result, peace eluded me. My sense of traction, decimated. I had become broken and disillusioned. The career I had so carefully built, trained toward, and fought to obtain was gone. When I looked in the mirror, I didn't recognize the old guy with the gray hair staring back at me. And so, as much as I wasn't interested in actually going to a Third World Country (not to mention a nation at war), I was desperately looking for something, a purpose that would make me feel alive again.

My wife Robbie, an incomparable woman of wisdom and support, spoke prophetic words that eventually coaxed me into accepting the invitation, "I feel that there's something for you in this trip."

I boarded the plane, still not convinced that she was right.

THE DARK CONTINENT

Sierra Leone is an African nation that almost succeeded in destroying itself. With one of the world's largest natural harbors, it was a port of entry for the transatlantic slave trade in its early known history. In 1787, some of London's "black poor," who had been promised freedom in exchange for service in the British Army, were dropped off on its coastline.

Five years later in 1792 through an arrangement with the Sierra Leone Company, Thomas Peters, a former slave, brought a second group of over 1,000 Black Americans. Together with other freed Africans, they established the capital city of Freetown. However, for the next 150 years it remained an unmanageable and impoverished British colony.

Its people finally won their independence in 1961, but since they had only known the bonds of slavery, they did not know how to maintain that freedom. Numerous military coups seized control until finally in 1991, a rebel group called the Revolutionary United Front (RUF) launched its first attacks. Liberia, a neighboring coastal country, assisted the RUF, and for the next eight years, parties warred to gain power.

Sierra Leone became the bloodiest nation in the world. The city of Freetown, once established in honor of freedom, received into its dust the highest number of massacred bodies in the whole nation. Two million people fled across its lands to refugee camps while the RUF, under the influence of drugs and terror, scoured and burned village after village. They cut off resisters' ears, arms, and even their legs. They stole young children fit for becoming child soldiers and forced capable men to pan for diamonds to support their importation of weapons. During this time, the nation's average lifespan dropped to 30 years.

As our plane landed, it was evident from my window that the airport had been battered by artillery. Dismal looking UN soldiers, charged with "keeping peace" greeted us as we stepped off the plane. No doubt behind their stoic appearances, they hid the emotion from having witnessed insufferable cruelty. Staring past their rigid figures, I could see that the country's natural beauty was astounding. Its tropical greenery and rugged mountains reminded me of the craggy brush and rock formations of coastal California.

I said little as our caravan (and UN escort) drove toward Freetown. War's evidence was laid bare everywhere. And on the road itself, demoralized men, women and children slowly trudged en masse toward the capital city, desperate for sanctuary. What they did not know was that the RUF were attempting to shut the city down.

We passed through several checkpoints. Grim military personnel holding machine guns checked every document thoroughly. I suddenly realized that if we made one wrong or impulsive decision, we could perish. The situation was beyond what I had imagined, and as I lay on my cot that night, with little power or water in our hotel and insects swarming the windows, I began to regret my decision.

What am I thinking?

But by the time I encountered the young girl who thrust her daughter into my arms, I thought, *How can I ever complain about my life again?* Their courage paled my own. The depth of their suffering completely stripped me of my self-pity. They had nothing, yet they rejoiced as if they had plenty. They had seen their families and villages annihilated, yet they were thankful for the little they had. On fifty acres, the refugee camps housed thousands of starving bodies. They lived in cardboard boxes, some with just a blanket for warmth. The camps were disease-ridden and lacking proper sanitation. Hundreds of amputees waited for prosthesis. I realized that before this moment, I hadn't known sorrow.

Yet there were also hopeful stories. On the coast, we visited an Italian priest who had established a safe camp for former child soldiers to help them deal with their emotional wounds. After being captured from their families, these boys, some as young as ten years old, had drugged and then forced to murder innocents. With this priest's courage and compassion, and global support from other Catholics, the camp housed hundreds of young men. The kitchen was only an open fire pit, and they lacked running water, but they had the richest gift of all, people that cared for and loved them.

As I moved past my self-absorption into their world, my mind cried out, *How can God handle this suffering?*

But as I witnessed the joy of the oppressed, the tenderness of Clive, the president of World Relief, and the Italian priest (not to mention the rest of my team), I realized that God had heard every single cry of the broken-hearted—the people I thought had been forgotten. He was using *us* to ease their pain.

WATERSHED

During my journey to Sierra Leone, I felt the gears shift into place. When I stepped outside of my own pain and witnessed the suffering of others, and in particular the young girl, I was not able to separate myself from her sorrow. I knew that my heart had finally been ripped open, and I had moved past my mind and into my emotions. The image of the young girl begging me to rescue her daughter has haunted me ever since. As she turned from me and walked away, fully believing that I would take her child, I continued to weep. She wanted to entrust her baby to me, but I couldn't do what she requested. At home in Omaha, I was a father to four children. I saw her pain. I wanted to help, but the matter was out of my hands. Finally after regaining composure, I handed her baby to the director of the refugee camp. That day I had faced an impossible situation my corporate success, connections, or wealth couldn't solve.

Sierra Leone was a watershed in my life. I had been a lower-middle class kid from Iowa who dreamed a daring dream of wealth and prestige. My drive to "be someone" quickly escalated me into being a senior level executive for corporations listed as the top 50 by Fortune Magazine. Money abounded (and so did my ego). I began to live the life I had vowed to have as a child. But what I could never admit to myself was that I felt I was a "poser," a man that believes he knows everything because he has reached the zenith of corporate success, but who is also scared to death he will be proved inadequate.

And so, when I encountered suffering in its most desperate form—the pleas of a broken young girl who wished a new life for her daughter, my journey toward selflessness became real. For the first time, I saw beyond myself. In fact, I was an emotional wreck, completely undone and unable to process what was occurring.

No longer was I the narrow-focused high flyer who was far removed from outside trauma, unable to come close enough to suffering to feel its unjust stench. The anxiety about my own progression and vitality was dispelled. I was experiencing suffering firsthand, and began to understand how my talent and connections could benefit others.

I was beginning a journey that is fundamental to any man, whether business executive or priest—to be trusted with the hearts of others.

QUESTIONS FOR REFLECTION

1. Have you had a watershed experience in your life? What has it revealed to you?

2. Have you allowed yourself to walk alongside those in need to share in their suffering? Why or why not?

CHAPTER 2

— Court Jester —

"With the greater part of rich people, the chief enjoyment of riches consists in the parade of riches."
ADAM SMITH [3]

"THE IMPRESSION I have of you is that you are a clown…a court jester."

"Excuse me?" The CEO stared at me in disbelief.

Four of us were standing in the Departures Terminal of the airport in Tucson, Arizona: my wife Robbie, the CEO, his wife, and me. A few minutes before, this CEO and his tempered wife had wheeled their luggage in our direction. The CEO vaguely recollected that we had attended the same business summit. It was an invitation-only three-day event. I had definitely noticed him as he walked around parading his accomplishments like a strutting peacock. At first glance his jeans and t-shirt granted him a casual demeanor, but it was obvious that he craved affirmation. I could see through his façade and I knew that inside he asked the age-old question so many men do, "Do I have what it takes to be the CEO of an important organization?" Clearly he didn't believe he did, otherwise he wouldn't have needed to gallivant.

The CEO's nonchalant and arrogant countenance reminded me of myself, or at least who I had been for most of my life. Seeing someone else play the part reminded me of how much I had changed. Yes, I had been *that* guy. I had lived the early years of my life with the underlying belief, "I need to prove I am worthy of recognition." I quickly became the typical *Fortune Magazine* executive who sought recognition, traveled, dined at fine restaurants, socialized with the elite, and outsmarted coworkers for position. My nickname? "Mr. Iceman." *Ouch.* It was all to counteract one lie that had been ingrained in me since childhood: *I am not included in the "circle of men."*

When the CEO had asked casually, "What is it, again, that you do, Mike?"

I responded, "I give people advice."

"Ah…" A moment of silence until it sunk in. I knew what was coming next. It had happened countless times, *What does it take to be successful? Give me the keys to wealth. Break it down for me so I can get there quickly. I want to know how you "arrived."*

"So…" he began, as if challenging me, "Can you help me?"

"That depends on you," I answered.

"What do you mean?" he asked, guardedly.

"Well," I continued, "Are you open to feedback?"

"Yes…well, all right. Let me have it, Mike." His eyes shifted nervously…but he didn't know I could tell. He was afraid of what I would say, but he would never admit it.

That's when I told him that he was a court jester. His wife's eyes immediately focused on me. She knew the truth. So did my wife. He would never *arrive* if his only purpose was to prove he was a capable CEO. His motivation had to be beyond himself, though it is a rare quality in today's executive world.

"You're not an effective leader. You give off the signal that the world revolves around you and that you're only looking out for yourself. That's not creating a safe environment for those around you."

He was stunned. I kept going, having reserved myself already for three days, "If you want to be a leader that people actually *want* to follow, you need to take a good look at yourself."

He laughed, trying to brush off the words, "You are pretty tough, Mike!" His body language said what he couldn't.

No doubt I hurt his pride, but I was running out of time. "Respect doesn't come from titles, pecking order or possessions."

Silence again. He didn't know how to respond.

Robbie tapped my arm. "It's boarding time."

I reached into my pocket and pulled out my business card, "Call me."

"Yeah, I'll call you." He laughed, waving me off.

Before I walked away, I made certain to catch his wife's eye. She knew I had pinpointed his motivation—the underlying belief that projected itself into every area of his life. Her eyes said it all; *He doesn't believe he has what it takes.* I wanted to give her hope. I had been there once…but I had also, changed.

THE VOW

I wish I could say that I woke up one day and was different. I wish I could say that I effortlessly stopped worrying about myself and lived for the benefit of others. Transformation is sometimes long-suffering, and my lack of confidence began as a young teenager.

My father "swore like a sailor," so to speak. Despite his rough exterior, he had a tender heart. Since he was an avid hunter and supporter of conservation and habitat preservation, local hunters and fisherman appreciated his friendship. On most evenings, we'd have townspeople at our house, telling stories of their latest outdoor adventures. Some of my favorite memories are those nights at supper. I also fondly remember filling shotgun shells, tying flies, hunting frogs at midnight, skinning rabbits, crawling along creek beds, and scaring pheasants so my father and his friends could shoot them from the riverbank.

My mother kept busy at home with three boys and five girls while my father ran a small heating and air-conditioning company. They never had much money, nor did they have aspirations of success. To them, the greatest ambitions of life were to raise their children well with good values, provide for them and love their neighbors. The fact that we weren't rich never seemed to bother them. In fact, I don't think that they thought about it. Wealth was simply outside of their world.

During my childhood, I can remember two pivotal events that shaped my future mindset. The first was an experience with my father.

"Mike!" My father yelled, clearly upset at me. He slammed his tools down on the worktable. We were in the basement of our client's house.

I snapped out of my daydream (probably about sports or girls) and looked at him, realizing I was caught. I could hear what he wanted to say in his voice. He had a strong work ethic, and I wasn't keeping up. What followed next, in a matter of thirty seconds, caused a deep wound inside of me. At thirteen, it became a defining moment.

He pointed his finger at me from across the room, "You had better get a good education, Mike, because you are not going to make a living with your hands!"

I was hurt and filled with shame, and began to believe a lie that I didn't belong. My father had showed me how to be a man by letting the wilderness or unknown test me, but what I heard in his comment was that I was being thrown out of his "circle of men." His words pulled me downward. He was telling me that I just "didn't have what it takes" to make it in his world. I wanted to work alongside him, but I knew I didn't meet his expectations. He was a blue-collar trade worker, and I didn't fit. I felt like I couldn't be who he wanted me to be, but instead of realizing that it was acceptable to have different dreams than him, I believed that I was less of a man.

On that day, I made a vow: *I will be more successful than all of them. I will be wealthy, powerful and create my own circle of men. I am not going to make a living with my hands. I will go the white-collar route and make more money than any of the men in Carroll, Iowa. My Dad is right, his life won't work for me.* That painful experience was the beginning of my quest to find a path on which I *did* belong.

Once I had decided that my father's way of life was not what I wanted, I lost value for his opinions, and started idolizing a man named Bill. Bill was pivotal experience number two. He was a dreamer who was confident he could attain beyond the status quo of Iowa. He started a small beer distribution company that quickly grew into a large tobacco, candy and snack company. By the time I was a teenager, he was one of the wealthiest men around.

Bill had a son my age, and he built a baseball field for him. Not only that, but he was also a catalyst for our town's urban renewal. He was the patron for a professional merchant baseball team. Our players were so talented that a few made it to the Major Leagues. As Bill's wealth increased, so did his influence, and when I was nine years old, I realized that he and his family were asked to be in the rich men's clubs that I would never be a part of—*unless* I became like him. I hadn't been allowed to enter the golf club with his son because I wasn't dressed properly. I never forgot the embarrassment, and I vowed that I would be a rich man privileged with elitism. The situation made me jealous enough to swear, *I am not going to think "small." I am going to do whatever it takes to get rich!* I coveted the power and influence Bill had, and I never wanted to worry about not having enough money.

I became fixated on creating wealth and achieving position. I wouldn't settle for my father's nine-to-five, hardworking, and middle class world. It was my way of showing everyone, including my father, that I was better than the rest. In high school, I took college preparatory courses instead of woodshop, and I began to research careers and companies that would provide the fastest route into the world of power and prestige. I began to build a pathway toward my future life. I calculated how I could find my way to the top of the business world. I strategically fit the puzzle pieces together, knowing that I would arrive at an untouchable and perfect image of what I should be: a well-groomed, sophisticated and wealthy man for whom others would work. By the time I left for college, my parents didn't understand me and I had stopped seeking advice from my father. He simply didn't know how to help me in my newfound ambition. I knew that if I wanted to make something of myself, as I had vowed, I was on my own. That was, at least, until I met a woman known by her nickname, "Bird."

QUESTIONS FOR REFLECTION

1. What vows (conscious or unconscious) have you made?

2. In what ways have they propelled your life in a positive or negative direction?

CHAPTER 3

— Holding Hands with Love —

"Those things which are precious are
saved only by sacrifice."
DAVID KENYON WEBSTER [4]

M Y FIRST STOP after Creighton University was Mutual of
Omaha. I had been offered a job as a Group Sales Repre-
sentative. One day, as I made my way around the tables at M of O's
cafeteria, my friend Sandy called out to me. "Hey Hotdog!" (Hotdog
was my nickname at college.) "I want you to meet someone," she
continued.

I didn't know what I was in for. But as I turned to look at the
woman standing next to her, I felt my knees almost give way. *Wow!*
I thought, but didn't let the weak feeling overcome me, or even
show. I had become efficient at pulling off my façade of "having
it together." There wasn't a need for me to be vulnerable…at least,
not yet.

She was tall and blonde with piercing blue eyes. A snow-white
smile and a radiance I couldn't quite put my finger on (not to
mention a mini skirt), made her seem *perfect*.

"Hotdog, meet Bird."

I said something entirely sarcastic (not knowing what else to say in her presence), "Bird? What kind of name is that?"

"Well what kind of a name is Hotdog?" she quipped in return.

It's difficult to explain, and some people call it cliché, but in that moment, I knew she was the woman for me. No question about it. We began to spend a lot of time together—at first, just as friends. In intelligence and wit, we were equals. But that was where the similarities ended. Whereas I was full of adventure and constantly looking for the next opportunity to conquer, Robbie was sensitive, compassionate, and wanted to establish a home and a family.

She was selfless where I was selfish, and because of that, I trusted her. I would call her for advice, and not much time passed before I knew needed her in my life continuously. We married soon after meeting, feeling like we had always known each other and that we were the only ones alive who could fill that role for one another.

WAKE UP CALL

Twenty years after that day in the cafeteria, the look on Robbie's face told me I had made a mistake—again. My greatest supporter was disappointed and hurt. By whom? Yeah, by me.

Great, I thought. *I did it again, didn't I?* As usual, I had informed, rather than included her in the decision that we needed to pack up our lives so that I could move up the corporate ladder. My next title would be Vice President of Consumer Products for the Walt Disney Company. In my mind, this was the best step toward my dream. It was the fall of 1992, and I had already opted out of three companies that hadn't presented me with the long-term opportunity I desired: Mutual of Omaha, General Mills, and PepsiCo. Disney was number four. Along the way we had birthed two children, Amber and Dustin. Amber was two years older than Dustin. She was a dancing queen, full of life, laughter and energy. Dustin was our more reserved, intuitive and creative musician. Our children were opposites and a beautiful addition to our family.

"Think of the movie premiers...the parties!" I emphasized. "We can even take the kids to Disneyland any time we want!" I said, hoping to convince her. I didn't want to look into her eyes. I was afraid of what I would see.

None of what I said mattered to her. She didn't care about affluence like I did. In fact, she didn't even have the *need* to care. I didn't know it at the time, but Robbie was secure in herself in a way I never had been. I *needed* a new and prestigious job to help me feel like a man. The unrelenting voice inside my head still told me that I wouldn't be included in the "circle of men" if I wasn't constantly moving up.

For years, Robbie had supported my desires while paying a price. Not only did she work full-time, but she was also an around the clock mom since I was often working too many hours or traveling. Essentially, she had been raising our kids on her own while I had laid down my life for position and promotion. The higher I moved up the corporate ladder, the more she was forced to sacrifice. Often my heart would remain at work after I arrived home. I was in perpetual motion, fixated on attaining a promotion, a bigger house, better cars and what I thought would be a better life. I became a stranger to my family and I could tell that Robbie was hurting inside.

She would tell me, but I couldn't understand. To me, *my* success was *our* success. Time and again I shut her out when she asked, "What is wrong with you? Is our life ever going to be something other than 'getting ahead?'"

"But Robbie, you are asking me for something I don't have. I am tired and don't have the energy to fix your problems after I've been dealing with everyone else's all day long." Instead of understanding her pain, I took her comments as a cut to my manhood. At my core I believed, "I don't have what it takes. I can't be what she wants."

Through the busyness and attempt to build my dream, we drifted apart. Finally in Hawaii on a rare vacation, she asked me, "Where is the 'Mike' I married? What happened to my awesome man?" Although we didn't know how to fix our marriage at the time, we both began to think, *There's got to me more than this.*

Robbie's questions shook me, and they caused me to realize I had become cold and disengaged. But instead of looking for a way to change, I became angry and frustrated with her. I couldn't give up my obsession with work, so I tried to find a way to juggle everything. Quitting was not an option. I pushed myself harder, believing that if I just kept going, I would eventually reach a plateau that housed everything I desired. That, however, was simply not possible. And the message I was sending to Robbie about the priority in my life was devastating to her. I didn't know how she felt at the time, but she interpreted my words as, "He's not going to be there...he's going to leave me." She began to attend classes at a local community college, believing that there would come a time that I would leave her, and she'd have to find a way on her own with two children. I had no idea that I was dangerously close to losing her.

Robbie knew that the unwritten rule at high levels in corporate America was that if your wife couldn't stomach the sacrifice, divorce her and look for someone who didn't care if she came second. Among the senior executives at my present company, I was the only one who was still married to his first wife. Despite my eagerness to sacrifice time for advancement, I knew that if there did come a moment when I would have to make a choice between Robbie and my career, I would choose her. But I never told her or let her know that she was my first priority. I assumed she already knew. I know now that one of women's greatest desires is to feel safe.

Two opposing sides, work and home, vied for my attention and I was struggling. When I would approach mentors, the implication was clear: "I will cut you some slack, Mike, but the expectations of your position are the same. You will have to figure this out yourself."

How Robbie and I arrived at this place, from feeling like we'd known each other our whole lives to living separately under the same roof, is a story in itself. Through it all my wife stood with me. She believed in me, even when she couldn't see the man she married in my eyes. There were seasons of intense arguing, but she hoped that if she continued to love me, we'd find a way to repair the damage that had been done.

What first initiated the change was the realization that a true husband and leader provides safety and promotes those above, beside, and below to flourish in *their* dreams. It seems like an obvious concept now, but at the time, the thought had never occurred to me. A leader who realizes, "It's not about me" can create an atmosphere in which others thrive. It's a strategic three-step process: provide, protect, and most of all *pray*. I did not attain this wisdom for a very long time, not until I had accomplished nearly all of *my* corporate aspirations. Yes, I had been *that* guy, just like the CEO who conspicuously strutted around his peers at the business summit. The conflict over moving from Orange County to L.A. so that I could work at Disney was the catalyst for the transformation we needed. Who knew that a foolish step could be used to initiate a life change so drastic that I would challenge the very lie I had built my life on?

QUESTION FOR REFLECTION

1. Have you put your needs above those you love? If so, what do you think you need to change?

CHAPTER 4

— The Most Dangerous —
Question

"The end of every maker is himself."
ST. THOMAS AQUINAS [5]

"THE ONLY WAY you'll know, man, is to ask her." Andy, my gruff-looking roommate during the Promise Keeper's conference, patted my shoulder affirmatively, as if what he was saying was easy to hear. [6]

I've never been one to flock to a men's meeting, or even participate in something that required inner reflection or emotion. But a brief amount of time at Disney changed my perspective. I had just turned forty and had begun to admit to myself, "I don't have it all together." For the first time, I began to ask, *Who are you, Mike?* After all my attempts to make something of myself, I still hadn't reached the man I thought I should be, and I certainly hadn't pleased my family. I knew God was asking me, "Are you at the end of your rope yet, Mike?" He wanted me to relinquish control. That was a lot to ask. I had come to the conference hoping to find "the answer."

So, there I was, sitting in a hotel room at a Promise Keeper's conference with a rough looking man I had just met, who was now giving me advice about my marriage. I never would have been caught in this situation, even a few months before. My roommate Andy was a man with far more courage than me at the time. He was a Puerto Rican ex-gang member who managed a self-storage unit. Because of his past, he was fearless. His presence impacted me because I wasn't intimidating to him. Here was a manly man who was not afraid of being vulnerable or showing love. To talk openly and honestly about God or even love was normal for him.

Andy carried on in his comforting street lingo, "It won't hurt to go home and face it."

I shook my head with a slight smile on my lips. He was challenging me to talk to Robbie, to actually *ask* her what her dreams were. It seemed like a simple task, but it terrified me.

Earlier, during that first night of the conference, former Coach Bill McCartney from the University of Colorado said to us, "Many people ask me why I left college football when I was at the top. The simple answer is that God ambushed me." A guest speaker at his church had challenged the men with a simple question, "Whose dreams are you living? Yours or your spouse's?" Bill was challenging us with that same question.

I felt convicted. It hit me in that instant that I had never paid attention to Robbie's dreams. I didn't even know what they were...

Coach McCartney continued, "In case you don't know, just look at your wife's countenance. You can tell if she is loved and happy by the look in her eyes."

Her eyes? Surely Robbie was happy...if she wasn't, I'd certainly been a selfish husband...was it possible that she wasn't happy? Oh my God...

"When I went home," Coach McCartney went on, "I found out

that my wife's dreams weren't college football. I had been living my dreams, not hers."

I have been so blind, I thought. It was time for me to take a look in the mirror. I never considered the possibility that her dreams might be different than mine. When we'd first met, I would talk about the future, and tell her, "I'm not going to work for this company forever…I'm moving on to bigger and better places." She'd look at me, her eyes sparkling, and I knew she was my biggest cheerleader. I figured that if I were happy, she'd be happy, and I assumed that she'd follow me anywhere. Now she had done so…for twenty years.

But Robbie hadn't dreamt about being married to a wealthy man who could offer her a privileged life. As a mid-western tomboy, she would have been happy raising cattle and children on a farm. Nonetheless, from the start of our lives together after Creighton, she acted as a partner to accomplish *my* dreams simply because she wanted me to be happy. We were traveling through life together, but our route had never readjusted to include any of her dreams…it had always been about *me*.

IN THE GAME

When Robbie and I were first married, we were a young couple living a dream. We both worked for Mutual of Omaha, which was the sponsor for *Mutual of Omaha's Wild Kingdom*, an extremely popular TV series that featured wildlife and was one of the first to promote ecological consciousness. As a company, M of O was a "kingdom" within itself, full of other young people, opportunity, and up and coming executives. Not long after being positioned in the Group Sales Department, I got my first glimpse at the under-belly of big business.

I was responsible for developing relationships with third party administrators who managed massive pension, health, and welfare plans for organizations such as the Teamsters and Longshoremen. The Teamsters was one of the most powerful unions in the United States. I was directed to keep people happy while solving potential crises. In one particular case, Corporate wanted an audit of some of the companies paying into the collective Teamsters' health and welfare plan. They wanted to know if we were receiving an accurate account of premiums. This was a normal practice for insurance companies, so M of O's corporate auditor and I arrived at the Teamster's headquarters to audit them.

The head of the Teamsters' Union found out what we had been commissioned to do. Supposedly he was the former bodyguard of Jimmy Hoffa, the Teamsters' President from 1958 to 1971. Before we could get to the point where we could prove something was a bit "fishy," two very large, hard-muscled men with fiery eyes and angry appearances walked toward us. They grabbed our arms and started to escort us toward the Exit sign. I was in shock, not fully gauging what was occurring until one of them growled, "Get the hell outta here! You will *not* audit the Teamsters!"

Since Hoffa had been convicted of attempted bribery of a Grand Juror, it was not surprising that the union closely guarded their territory. Once I found out that my boss wouldn't cross the union leadership, I knew that I would need to be shrewd if I wanted to get the job done. I was beginning to understand that ambition wasn't enough.

The 1970s were also a critical point of change in business protocol. Employees were no longer the foremost interest in company management. Rather, it became quarterly earnings. Employees were now an "expense." Profit took precedence over relationship. Loyalty was becoming a thing of the past, and people could not expect to work for the same company their entire life.

In light of this, I learned to have thick skin and an aggressive nature. I strategized to find the right connections, and would ask the question, "Can this person help me advance?" If the answer was, "No," I'd move on to someone else. I started to become highly competitive and left my parents' core values behind. I became a pro at conflict management, hiring and firing. I could dangle a carrot to obtain results without being bothered by morale. If someone did not produce for me, it was simple—that person held no value. I overshadowed my peers in Human Resources, especially since empathetic women had historically dominated HR, and I soon became impatient with M of O. I was confident I could play the game of big business, but I wasn't about to wait around to get promoted.

ON AND UP

When General Mills offered me a managerial position in HR I took it. General Mills was a hundred year-old Fortune 500 Company experiencing exponential growth. I arrived at the perfect time. In 1980, after recruiting talent from the nation's top universities, General Mills diversified beyond Wheaties, Cheerios and Betty Crocker into multiple industry lines. They bought restaurant chains like Red Lobster and Olive Garden, toy brands such as Parker Brothers, specialty retailing like Eddie Bauer, and even IZOD with its green alligator logo.

I found myself working with top executives from General Mill's five industries and I learned each of their business models. I knew that if I played smart, and was loyal and willing to sacrifice, I would move upward. It only took three years before corporate asked me to be the Director of Personnel for IZOD. Our little green alligator was everywhere at the time, and I took the opportunity with pride. My new workplace was on Seventh Avenue in New York, NY. This was Manhattan, and my office was on the same street that was familiarly called "Fashion Avenue." Near us were Carnegie Hall, NY's most notable concert venue; Penn Station, the major intercity train station; and Madison Square Garden, the longest active major sporting facility in the New York Metropolitan area. It was a giant adventure and a whirlwind of new experience that kept me interested. I loved every moment, and I knew it was only the beginning.

Unfortunately, we were growing so quickly that our infrastructure couldn't keep up. Despite my attempts at organization, recruiting new hires, and working over the top, our sales began to slide after the first year. We were forced to downsize, and I knew I wasn't interested in working on another spin off. I wanted a better position. I wouldn't feel like I had arrived in the "circle of men" until I had reached the top.

Since I had become recognized by my efforts at General Mills, headhunters knew me well and I received a call from PepsiCo in 1984. As the world's largest beverage and snack food company, it had a reputation for being fast-paced and driven by high performance. It was a company in which I could develop quickly, ideal for a competitive achiever without an ounce of humility. I soon became the quintessential poster-boy for PepsiCo. I was smart, athletic, and articulate—the perfect candidate to mold into what they wanted. A few months into PepsiCo, I was moved to Dallas, TX as Frito Lay's (a subsidiary of PepsiCo) Director of Human Resources.

I was in my thirties and already on my way to becoming a Vice President of Frito Lay. I positioned myself for what I wanted. I knew I needed to "manage up" and make those above me not only appreciate my influence, but begin to need me in order to accomplish something. I knew who could do the most for me, and I catered to them, helping them believe I had earned the privilege to be on the top level.

QUESTIONS FOR REFLECTION

1. What is the driving force in your life?
2. How has it affected those you love?

CHAPTER 5

— Green Card —

*"The heart is forever making
the head its fool."*
FRANÇOIS DE LA ROCHEFOUCAULD [7]

M Y EFFORT at Frito Lay paid off and I soon got the "green card" from my boss.

"Mike, you have incredible capacity. You have potential, and we believe you will go places."

Green meant: "Go to the top! You are part of the long-term team. You have the skill, ambition and commitment to make it into the top executive club. You will make millions…!"

My new color code superseded those of Blue, Yellow and Red. "Blue" meant you would stay where you were. "Yellow" meant that you had hit your ceiling, and "Red" meant that your time had elapsed and you were out of the game.

No one above you was allowed to tell you your "color," but with that comment from my boss, I knew I was "green." It fueled my fire. The questions I had been asking inside about my identity were getting answered. I felt like a race horse clamoring at the gates, ready to be let loose to run and perform. I didn't realize that I had become obsessed. My value was dependent on how fast and how far I could go. I even carried a little card in my pocket that identified the total compensation package at the highest level, Level 30. Top executives participated in long-term programs such as stock options and stock appreciation, performance shares, club memberships, not to mention…fancy cars.

I learned how to develop those under me, though at this point I still didn't care too much for other people's aspirations. Profits and market shares were always top priority. Developing leaders was for the purpose of replacing yourself and making more money for the company. I was adept at evaluating whether or not middle managers were worth developing within minutes, and if they were, I would sculpt them to lead thousands. If people didn't fit, their time with the company would be over. It was never personal. It was business.

A few years later in 1989, I was told, "Mike, we need you at Taco Bell in Irvine, California."

Another move, but the Vice President position felt even more possible with the sacrifice. No doubt I proved myself again. Within a year, Taco Bell transformed from a sleepy Mexican restaurant to one of the top five fast-food chains in the United States. We caught mainstream attention through national advertising campaigns such as "Run for the Border."

At Taco Bell I was responsible for identifying, grooming and placing executive leadership within the company. I didn't even have to do it on my own. My superior, Bill, was also grooming me as an executive. He believed in me and I catered to his admonitions, seeking affirmation and applause.

In his early fifties, Bill understood that if he could do something for me, I could do something for him. His job was to groom me to become an effective leader who produced well. Whatever he asked me to do, I did: buy new clothes, create a "presence," position yourself, present yourself well, become emotionally unattached, cultivate self-efficacy, take more responsibility, and attend executive management courses at Stanford.

He would tell me, "Mike, at Level 16, the company is interested in results. If you can't do it, they'll find someone who can."

Essentially, I was being asked to lay my life down for Taco Bell, and I did. I knew that without him I could be permanently shelved. Thankfully, Bill was positioning me in the company and his influence could take me exactly where I wanted to go.

That was my plan until the day I found out that Bill had been promoted to Corporate in New York.

DOWNTURN

Bill's replacement was someone who lacked leadership skills, and frankly, I didn't respect him. The day he walked into my office, his attitude told me, "You might have been Bill's Golden Boy, but you are not mine." He was arrogant, and I detested his attitude.

My first assignment for him was to fire Bill's long time secretary.

"Why exactly do you want me to fire her?"

He shrugged nonchalantly, "I just want someone else."

Any ounce of respect I might have had for him was gone. Bill's secretary was considered one of Taco Bell's top employees and she had dedicated heart and soul to the company for decades. She would never make an equivalent wage elsewhere.

When I was forced to tell her, she asked, "Why does he hate me?"

It didn't stop there. Don (a new PepsiCo Executive well known by his previous experience as the president of Denny's) and I were in the midst of setting up a company within Taco Bell. We booked time for the team at a resort in Big Sur, California. Having heard of our plans, our new boss barged in during one of our meetings. "I just heard you guys are going to Big Sur. That's over the line! You shouldn't be using money for that, especially at your position."

Don immediately quipped back, "Who are you to tell us what to do? This is in our budget, not yours!"

Then came the moment that led me to the end of my time at Taco Bell—I chose Don's side of the argument. I knew it was over. I had lost my mentor Bill, and with him the ability to arrive at the top. Up until then, I had enjoyed my time at the company, but everything I had built came tumbling down. It was not supposed to happen, and I didn't have a backup plan. Within months, I let headhunters know my availability. That's when I got the call from the Walt Disney Company in Burbank, California.

My exit didn't exactly occur in the way I had anticipated. In fact, it was painful. Through my constant scheming for position, I had sowed mistrust with my coworkers. On my last day, I arrived at a meeting and was surprised to realize that no one was sorry I was leaving. They were cold and unfeeling. I was shocked, though I should have known. I had always played the game selfishly. Even though I was in the business of developing people, I really didn't care about anyone else's potential, only if they held the means to get me where I wanted to go. This was the first glimpse of misfortune that caused me to think, *My life isn't working.* My life slammed on the break pedals, but I wanted to keep moving up. The pathway before me came to a halt without my permission.

QUESTIONS FOR REFLECTION

1. Is your life "working?"

2. If the answer is "No," what adjustments might you need to make to get on track again?

CHAPTER 6

— The Question —

"It is only through the surrender of our mind's ideals
that we enable our hearts to thrive, and through our hearts'
thriving we attract the success that previously eluded us."
VANESSA J. CHANDLER [8]

I WAS TERRIFIED that night. I was about to do what my roommate Andy had challenged me to do at Promise Keeper's. I couldn't get the thoughts out of my mind and if Robbie had bad news for me, I wanted to get it over as quickly as possible.

"What are your dreams, Robbie?" I exhaled the words lightly, as if it would be less painful to say them in that manner.

She was not prepared. She stared at me blankly. I felt my heart beat wildly in expectation. I was hoping that I hadn't been as selfish as I thought.

"*Why* are you asking me this?" she finally responded, somewhat perturbed.

"I want to know what your dreams are," I stated, feeling quite proud that I had accomplished the challenge. I knew I was about to be rewarded. Her dreams couldn't be that far off from mine.

"I want more children…and I want to live near my parents in Omaha."

Wait a minute! Now it was my turn to be utterly shocked. My worst fears were confirmed! I felt sick inside. Her sacrifice finally made sense. Move after move, position after position. She had given up everything and tried to tell me in the process, but I simply hadn't…*listened.*

"I've been trying to tell you this for years, Mike!" she went on. "Haven't you been listening?"

I could hear the anger in her voice. I hadn't heard her. How could I have been *that* guy? The selfish, hotheaded man who doesn't know anyone least of all himself…

I had arrived at a moment of revelation where either ignoring the truth or turning back would only amplify my struggle. When I began my position at Disney and attended the Promise Keeper's conference, it wasn't the end of my search for wealth and affluence. But it was the end of believing sacrifice was an easy burden. Robbie wasn't thriving and I finally realized it was my fault. It was time for me to examine myself in the mirror, one of the most difficult tasks a man can undertake. I had to face myself and ask, *Who are you? Where are you going?* And most painfully, *How can you give back to your wife?* As humbling as it was to let down my walls of self-sufficiency, I needed to be vulnerable with Robbie. I needed her more than ever because I was reaching the end of myself, and I began to wonder if at one time or another, we all come to the crossroad where we are given an opportunity to make a better choice.

RESTORING RELATIONSHIP

Something new had begun. It was more of an internal sense than logic, a knowing that caused me to take risk and even potentially sacrifice my career. From my frame of reference, that knowing is the Spirit of God. I don't understand how I became a new Mike Frank, but I did not doubt that this Spirit was responsible for the journey. Not only that, but I had more peace than ever before. I was becoming satisfied, not only from external blessing, but because I knew that the decisions I was making were right.

I'd like to say that I came in contact with the Spirit by my own initiative. But the knowing began after the first life-threatening event that happened in my family. Our eldest child, Amber, started attending a local church's youth group. Although she would come home from meetings full of life and enthusiasm, I did not pay too much attention to what was happening inside of her because I already considered our family "Christian." Nevertheless, Robbie and I decided to attending a couple's home group. Not only were the people in the home group vocationally successful, but they also had the same family values with which Robbie and I were raised. Their kindness surprised me, and their love for people other than themselves was something I had not often witnessed in the corporate world.

On one particular weekend, Amber went on a camping trip with her youth group. Our son Dustin, two years younger than Amber, was staying with friends. Robbie and I decided to go country western dancing, but as soon as we entered the dance hall, one of the employees found us, "Are you Mike and Robbie Frank?"

The minute he asked the words my heart started to pound.

"There was a phone call for you."

This was the moment every parent dreads. I was deathly afraid that something had happened to one of my children. When the employee handed us the name and number of the parents of one of Amber's friends, my worst fear was confirmed. I immediately dialed the number and tried to hold myself together.

"Mike, the kids have been in a bus accident," the father who answered the phone said.

I swallowed and braced myself, "Is Amber okay?"

"I don't know yet. All I know is that the bus drove down a steep embankment. Helicopters airlifted some of the kids out, but the hospital in Palm Springs won't disclose any information until you arrive. You need to call the hospital immediately."

I imagined the worst. *What if Amber is dead?*

The hospital informed me that she was alive, but they would not give any more information, "Yes, Mr. Frank, the bus your daughter was on was in an accident. She was airlifted out and you need to come right away."

I felt tears sting my eyes, but they refused to break through the wall I had created so that I wouldn't fall apart. "Please tell me if my daughter is okay," I begged. By that time Robbie was crying, and I felt I needed to keep it together for her sake.

"We will give you all the information when you get here," was the solemn reply.

The drive to Palm Springs felt far too long. My imagination played through fond memories with my daughter. Amber was Daddy's girl. We had a special relationship. What would I do without her? Holding back tears and smiling to myself, I thought of her dressed in Indian garb, sitting around the campfire during our trip with the Indian Princess Organization. She and I took the trip together, father and daughter. Her Indian name was Shooting Star, and I was Baboon Arising (instead of "Bad Moon Rising," a song by Credence Clearwater Revival). What a beautiful image! Amber was my only girl. I loved her dearly…and if she was taken from my life, how would I ever recover? I had never before been faced with such desperate fear. My body trembled as I pleaded with a distant God. I even made vows of all the things I would change if He would simply keep Amber alive.

As soon as we entered through the sliding glass doors of the emergency room, we saw many of our friends from the home group. I was grateful to be surrounded by familiar faces. One of the fathers came up to us with a smile. "Amber's going to be fine. Don't worry."

Robbie erupted with tears again, and heightened by adrenaline, I focused on trying to relax. There was no other explanation for Amber's survival except for a miraculous intervention by God, and He was beginning to command my respect. The doctors had simply been waiting to release Amber, and she walked out to us in a hospital gown. She was a bit wobbly, but safe, minus a broken wrist and a bandage on her head.

Investigation proved that not only did the bus driver have cocaine in his system, but he had also redirected his eyes to read a map. The bus ran off the road, rolled over completely three or four times, and slid down a ravine. Only a large ledge of rocks had stopped it from rolling down the 1500-foot drop.

As I hugged my daughter, the significance of the moment overcame me. I was a blessed man. Death had never before threatened to take someone so close to my heart. I had been terrorized with guilt. How could I have let her go? I felt this had been my fault. Not only that, but before Amber left on her trip, I had said, "Goodbye," to her casually, fully expecting that I would see her again. After the superficial acknowledgment, my mind instantly reverted back to the other tasks at hand. Relationship, even with my family, was secondary to the events and pursuits of my professional career. I took my family for granted. I was astounded at my blindness and that I had lived this way for so long.

Experiencing a life-threatening event shifted my focus, and I began to ask, "What is most important in life?" Though I no longer doubted that the Spirit was leading me, it took several years before I surrendered control. I hadn't even begun to be tested. Would I still follow the Spirit if it meant I wouldn't reach my career goals? What if I were asked to surrender everything?

QUESTIONS FOR REFLECTION

1. Do you need to let go of controlling your life? Why or why not?

2. What would you be willing to do for your family's wellbeing?

CHAPTER 7

— In Wonderland —

"Not until we are lost do we begin to understand ourselves."
HENRY DAVID THOREAU [9]

M Y STINT at Disney was not drawn-out. It didn't take me long to realize, "I made a mistake by coming." The experience at Promise Keepers altered my perspective of family and the role I must take to help my wife and children succeed. Initially, I had been seduced by Disney's glamour, but very soon I was falling down Alice's hole into a world I knew very little about.

Instead of reveling in the title of Vice President, I was just another player in a very large corporation, and if I didn't play by the pre-established rules I would be out. I was confined to doing everything by the book to avoid lawsuits. Further complicating my job was a lack of a long term plan to develop employees. This was a short-term culture, and once a movie or project was complete, people were terminated. If people produced well, they'd be applauded and in the spotlight...for a season. They didn't value Human Resources because of their short-term mentality. There was always talent that would accept short-term work. Disney never made developing people a focus because they didn't have to. My years of learning and developing as an executive were not useful. Little attention was given to my expertise. I was merely an executive with a title who had minimal authority.

FOLLOWING THE INNER VOICE

When I first made the decision to leave Disney, a mentor pleaded with me, "Mike, I appreciate the fact that you want to honor your wife and maybe the start-up will work. But if you stay at Disney you will be first in line for the best jobs in the country! If you move to Omaha…well who knows? You will be forgotten!"

To my amazement, only a week after I first talked to Robbie about her dreams, MFS Communications recruited me. Yes, it involved risk. A large percentage of start-ups never make it. Surprisingly, MFS offered me more compensation than I was making at Disney plus stock in the company. I was ready for this wild ride, and couldn't believe I was about to be financially rewarded for taking my family on an adventure.

MFS was a group of smart engineers. Not only did I like them, but I also respected them. This brought me peace and excitement about MFS's possibilities. They saw opportunity where others saw risk, and they knew that the Internet world would soon explode. They were also friends of Warren Buffet, the second wealthiest man in the world at the time, which meant that MFS would be well funded.

Up to that point, MFS was an unknown. More than one coworker had chastised me, "Mike, are you sure you want to do this? Going to Omaha is career suicide!"

It could have been career suicide, but at Disney I had finally begun to see that my family needed to be given a chance to live their dreams. By no means had I hit the ceiling of my potential as an executive, but I had stopped growing internally, and once I asked Robbie that most dangerous question, I knew it was time to save my marriage. I was becoming a new Mike Frank. I knew the move would be risky, but I also knew that it was time to end my single-minded pursuit of wealth. I overlooked the snide remarks like, "Farmer Mike!" and remained focused. I had a *knowing*, which I can only attribute to God, that Disney was the wrong place for my family and me. The prestige, wealth, and title Disney offered paled in comparison to my desire to change and follow the inner voice inside that told me to honor Robbie. I was determined to regain my family's love as a father who was present in both mind and heart.

SURRENDER EQUALS PAYOFF

Wall Street and the Associated Press heralded us as brilliant. Even Bill Gates, Microsoft's famous Chairman and CEO, was a player in our strategic alignment. It was 1995, and I was involved in one of the largest mergers of the decade. Our small MFS Communications corporation was about to purchase UUNET Technologies and create one of the world's premiere business communications companies. It would provide a single source for Internet, voice, data and video services through its advanced international fiber network. AT&T, MCI, Sprint, WorldCom all scratched their heads in wonder, "Who in the world is MFS Communications? Do *you* know who they are?"

"I think they are from Omaha..."

"Omaha? As in Omaha, *Nebraska*?"

"They spent two billion?"

"On *what* exactly?"

With the merger, we would become the only Internet service provider to own and control the fiber optic local loop, and intercity and subterranean facilities in the United States, United Kingdom, France and Germany.

Bill Gates stated,

> Our relationship with UUNET has been extremely positive over the past year and they have helped us deploy the Microsoft Network rapidly and with high quality. We are highly supportive of this merger with MFS, since combination of a facility-based telecommunications carrier with a high quality Internet service provider offers the potential for high bandwidth availability at lower costs for end users. [10]

With all that had happened, I couldn't deny that God was influencing my life. Yes, I was savvy, and had worked for years to establish myself as an executive, but I was coming into the *perfect* place at the *perfect* time. If I hadn't gone to Promise Keepers I may have missed out on one of the most significant opportunities of my life. What had felt like sacrifice was actually the leading of a divine voice. I used to say, "I'm just a lucky guy." But in this situation, luck was far too small of an influence. God was steering my family's course to bring us together *and* help our dreams come true. But it wasn't until I left the "land of dreams" that I finally felt that my family's wellbeing and our dreams were in alignment. I began to wonder, *Am I ready to surrender it all?*

I was about to find out.

TEST OF FAMILY

The *knowing* convinced me to leave Disney, but initially, moving back to Omaha had been Robbie's idea. What a surprise it was for Robbie when, a year after arriving back in Omaha, I took her on a coffee date and commented, "I don't think I'm done having kids."

"What?" Robbie was stunned at first, but she quickly grinned and laughed. "My husband wants more children?" she teased.

I hadn't forgotten her dream. That alone planted trust in my wife's heart that I had truly changed. It wasn't that I was particularly passionate about having another child, but I knew that Robbie's dream had been two-fold: move closer to her parents and have more children. I also knew that the Spirit was urging me to follow through, and that I could trust Him. I had an ideal career, and we were also financially set. Robbie was just over forty, but healthy and happier than I had seen her in a long time. There wasn't any reason why we shouldn't have more children.

Robbie stopped bantering with me and looked into my eyes. I could tell that her emotion was heightened, "Are you serious, Mike?"

I smirked playfully, "Let's have more kids!" And it was set. The happiness of our new life hit home while at a University of Nebraska football game with a friend.

"Robbie's pregnant," I said with a sense of pride. I felt great.

My friend laughed in surprise. "Don't you think it's a little late for that?" Then he continued, "Mike, you are a fortunate man. You work for a wonderful company, your wife is happy and you have a child on the way. How cool is that?"

He was right. I was a fortunate man. I wasn't worried about my future. It was formulaic really: follow the Spirit and He will work out everything in your life. Doing everything right equaled an expected outcome. "Bad" things occurred when something had been done in the wrong way.

However, just two weeks after our son Christian was born, my perspective of "expecting an easy life" was challenged. After visiting Robbie's sister in Springfield, Missouri, Robbie's parents were driving home to Omaha, but they never made it. A car hit them head-on and Robbie's dad died instantly. Her mother survived, but was put in intensive care.

Robbie's heart was overwhelmed with pain. She couldn't make sense of what had happened and would ask, "Why did you take my dad so soon, God? We just got back here...." Not only was Robbie mourning, but she was also taking care of our newborn, our other two children, and now her mother. I didn't have a grid for suffering. I didn't know how to comfort Robbie. Instead, I took care of the funeral details: I picked out the caskets, wrote checks, and organized the service.

Robbie had always been the one to go deeper with God, but the only thing I knew to do was read Scripture. What I found was different than the picture-perfect life I had imagined. I knew I needed to develop a deeper relationship with God, because I didn't know anything else that could carry us through. I couldn't walk through difficult situations on my own. I wanted to learn how to depend on His strength.

QUESTIONS FOR REFLECTION

1. Has an "inner voice" been speaking to you?

2. What might it prompt you to do?

CHAPTER 8

— Test of Honor —

"Who sows virtue reaps honor."
LEONARDO DA VINCI [11]

S HE WAS IN pristine condition, expensive, red-hot and gaining age. She was my ultimate dream. She was a 1967 Corvette Stingray Convertible.

There have been several instances in my career since Disney in which I learned to place the highest value on family and relationship. But could I actually value my wife's opinion above a childhood dream?

Sid Dillon was known as one of Omaha's most successful car dealers, and he happened to serve on the same non-profit board as me. Ironically, I had questioned a man once for "giving his time away for free," but through my involvement with the board, I was learning that there was value in serving others, even if it was "pro bono," or for the good of the people.

One afternoon while sitting in Sid's office, I noticed two miniature replicas of the 1967 Corvette on a shelf behind his desk.

"You know, Sid, I've always wanted to have a corvette like that," I said casually, pointing to his replicas.

"Oh yeah?" He laughed. "You are not going to believe this, but I have both of those cars out back…and one of them is for sale."

I nearly jumped out of my seat, "You're kidding!"

"Nope," he said with a grin. "Which would you like? Red or green?"

Uh-oh, I thought. *I shouldn't have opened up my mouth. Now I won't be satisfied until I've bought it!* Instead of voicing my thoughts, I shook my head and said, "I can't believe this!"

She was a beauty, a striking convertible with less than 60,000 miles. There wasn't a ding, nick or dent on her. She had always been garaged and hadn't even been wet underneath, a miracle for the Midwest.

I was sold immediately. I offered Sid an agreeable amount and I was about to sign the papers, but hesitated. Would I do business as usual and make my own decision, or would I talk to Robbie and allow her to be part of the decision? The green light inside urged me onward, "Go on. Just get the car!" I took it for a test drive and I was hooked! But I couldn't do it, so I raced home elated at the possibility of another dream fulfilled.

Could it get any better? I thought. It was as if she had been waiting for me for a very long time.

"That's nice, honey," Robbie responded, slightly on edge.

That's nice?!? I repeated in my mind. *She's not getting me. She just doesn't understand.* "I really want this, Robbie. Sid is giving me an excellent deal."

"Mike, it's not a good time. We really don't have space for it and given the weather, you would only be able to drive it a bit longer this year." She didn't have a need for the "thrill of the hunt" like I did. In her mind it was a waste, despite the fact that we had plenty of money to afford it. For her, it was just another toy that we'd have to take care of.

I tried to see things from her perspective. She was raising three kids; she cooked dinner every night, did the laundry for all of us and performed dozens of other daily duties. She probably felt like she would have to take care of the car while I was off being an "important business executive."

I was standing in the center of a crossroad. Robbie was forcing me to notice *how* I made decisions, and if I would choose *her* above an ideal possession. She didn't have to say the words, but I knew she was wondering if I would display my love through trusting her... instead of my egotistically driven desires. I knew she would accept my decision either way, but if I chose the car she wouldn't feel respected.

"Just go down there and drive it, Robbie. You'll see!"

I convinced her to test-drive it, but she remained firm. After feeling sorry for myself, I finally relented. Having a red-hot sports car without Robbie's approval would take away the pleasure of owning it. It wouldn't be worth it. I was still daydreaming about the car a few weeks later, and even prayed fervently I would forget the impossible to-find Stingray. Despite the disappointment, however, I knew I had made the right decision because it hadn't been defined by my bank account. It had been defined internally, and I had honored Robbie's request.

A few weeks later I got a call from my eldest child Amber, who owned a coffee shop at the time, "Hey Dad, can you come down here and sign some papers for me?'

"Sure. I'll be right there."

As I rounded the corner toward her coffee shop, my heart sank.

There in the parking lot was the 1967 red-hot Stingray. Somebody else had bought my dream car. It was too late. The dream was dead. I was immensely disappointed.

Before I reached the door of the coffee shop Robbie and Amber came running outside, grinning profusely.

I was clueless. "What's going on?"

Robbie grabbed me and laid a heavy kiss on my lips, "Happy anniversary, Honey!"

Wait a minute! I didn't know how to react. First I laughed. Then I smiled. I couldn't believe it. My wise and prudent, never whimsical wife had bought me my dream car. She already had it licensed and insured. All I had to do was get in and turn on the ignition.

"Here are the keys, Sweetheart." Her smile appeared to be permanent.

Then the tears threatened. *Me*—the guy who didn't like being vulnerable, especially in front of others. I couldn't stop smiling. This was so out of character for Robbie. I had given up the idea of the car to God, but He spoke to Robbie and put it back in my hands. When I got inside the car, I could feel Robbie's pleasure. *This is how it's supposed to be between a man and woman,* I thought. I realized that by honoring Robbie in something seemingly insignificant, our marriage had turned a corner. Why hadn't I figured this out earlier? Marriage wasn't about each of us giving 50-50. It was about each of us giving 100, more than enough, over and above so that our "love tanks" and marriage prospered in ways we could only dream. True love and intimacy with my wife would not come through method or schedule. It would come from choosing to go beyond what was expected at unexpected moments.

If I had been stubborn and simply done what I wanted to do, I might have lost something far more precious than 350 horsepower under the hood. I might never have learned the value of honoring my wife and the way it would make me, and our marriage feel—alive, just in the way we had been all those years ago when I'd first heard the name, "Bird."

QUESTIONS FOR REFLECTION

1. Evaluate your definition of honor: do you value "toys" or financial success above relationship with your family?

2. Which career goals would you have to give up if you surrender to something greater?

CHAPTER 9

— The Merger of the Century —

"Despite the nightmarish ending to the WorldCom saga,
the story had a fairy-tale beginning."
MICHAEL DESENNE [12]

I N THE FALL of 1996, the U.S. Federal Government was about to deregulate the telecommunications industry as soon as President Bill Clinton signed the bill. In the '80s, the government split the telephone industry into local and long distance service. AT&T, MCI, WorldCom and Sprint monopolized long distance service; AT&T's eight subdivisions, the Baby Bells provided local service. Customers chose both a local and long distance carrier, but this caused a disadvantage to the Baby Bells. Regulations dictated that they provide local service wherever people lived, even if there was only one client who lived in the country. As a result, residential phone service never profited except through large commercial or governmental accounts. This was where MFS came in. We strategically targeted large commercial and government accounts so that we wouldn't have the dead weight of nonprofitable residential customers.

In Washington DC we retained a lawyer so that new laws would favor MFS. The Baby Bells had brand recognition, and we didn't. But we built fiber optic rings around the financial centers of twenty-six major cities and essentially stole the Baby Bell's profit. Fiber optics (rather than copper) gave us the ability to offer higher speeds at a reduced cost. It didn't make sense for the Baby Bells to pull up the copper wire because so much money had already been invested. Not only did we sell better and faster phone service to commercial and governmental customers, but we also contracted long-distance carriers to bring in calls that we would switch to our fiber optic lines.

Of course the Baby Bells brought claims against us, stating that they were at a disadvantage because residential service wasn't profitable. People like Michael Powell, Chairman of the Federal Communications Commission, saw technological advancements such as ours and suggested that everyone compete under certain criteria. Deregulation was what we desired, but not for the reason most assumed. We wanted to sell MFS at a premium price and deregulation would cause companies to compete for our assets. Other executives and I held stock in the company. I had never been a part of something so potentially profitable and I was astounded at how it had all come to pass. We would be rich overnight.

Giving heed to what was ahead, MFS decided to purchase UUNET. UUNET was a group of young and geeky engineers from Fairfax, Virginia, who had figured out a way to make the Internet accessible to the broad public. In 1995, they were some of the first "techies" to be glorified before it became trendy. Their technology took the Internet out of dial-up service and provided the almost instant movement of data traffic. UUNET cost us two billion dollars, but we knew that with our fiber optic wires and their instant data transfer, MFS's value would become exponential.

A NEW GENERATION CORPORATE EMPLOYEE

"Guys," I said, barely able to keep myself from grinning in irony, "I need to talk with you."

Blank stares and seeming indifference. These geeky engineers from UUNET were a new generation that didn't necessarily aim to "arrive" but rather to "become." Their attire included grungy clothes and ACDC t-shirts. Almost anything was permissible by excuse of "inducing creativity," including Ping-Pong tables, leftover pizza boxes, and an office that looked like a pigsty.

"What's up?" one of them finally volunteered.

I looked at the floor. *Here I go…*

Starting with, "I've gotten a request from your coworkers," I explained that we needed to have a more "professional" dress code.

Moans, followed by grunts.

I jumped in laughing, "I hate to say it but the women are tired of seeing hairy armpits all day long!"

I was learning fast. This new generation of technology workers had Michael Dell, Bill Gates and Steve Job's paving the way to significance with remarkable payoff. Steve Jobs offered John Scully, PepsiCo's president and dynamic marketing executive, a place in a small and unknown company at the time: Apple. What could possibly entice a man who had reached earthly success (as defined by many) to leave everything behind? Scully was caught when Jobs prodded him with, "Do you want to sell sugar water for the rest of your life or do you want to come with me and change the world?" [13]

Like Jobs and Gates, many technological geeks in this new generation could become multi-millionaires in their twenties if they were successfully innovative. They weren't driven by fear, nor could money or power tempt them to surrender their talent and creativity. If I wanted to recruit the best technology "rock stars," I'd have to surrender my generation's ideal of buttoned-up, suit-wearing, and in their minds "boring" rich men, and meet them on their ground. I'd have to buy them the latest digital toys and provide a substantial budget, and I'd have to help them believe that they were working on the "cool," cutting edge projects.

Despite the small awkward confrontations about such things as "hairy armpits," I loved my job. I was hired to merge two worlds together. My leaders who were realistic and pragmatic gave me freedom. "We're not creating a postal system here, Mike. We don't want grade levels or detailed job descriptions. We are in uncharted waters. What it looks like today will not be what it looks like tomorrow. Just shape it as it grows."

From 1994 to 1997, I helped lead the company's expansion from less than 100 to more than 6,000 employees. Every day the fresh environment provided an exciting atmosphere in which to grow. Most importantly, my idea of "success" was being redefined, my wife was thriving and my children were happy. Things weren't how they had appeared to be in the past. What I thought would leave me behind actually propelled me forward. I gave up my reputation, financial status and "toys" to let my wife and children live their dreams. I traded "pedigree" for something that would change the world. Life was good, but I had yet to experience one of life's huge learning curves—suffering.

NASDAQ HISTORY

By 1996 we had molded MFS into a greatly coveted telecommunications company. That was our goal. We wanted to sell MFS at its peak and then move on to the next most profitable venture. WorldCom, a 100 billion dollar company, offered $14.2 billion, which was the highest bid so far. They were ambitious. They wanted everything from the ability to monopolize the local and long-distance providers to our customers and network.

We agreed, again through the recommendation of Bill Gates, and sold MFS to WorldCom. At the time, the sale marked the largest acquisition in NASDAQ history. The NASDAQ is the second-largest stock exchange market in the world. The media celebrated the merger. Again, we were the enigmatic company that surprised everyone.

"Who is MFS, again?"

"Some IT boys from Omaha."

"But why would WorldCom pay $14.2 billion?"

"Well, they see the potential of dominating the telecommunications industry. It would be a major stepping stone!"

I couldn't believe it! Not only was work fun and challenging, but I was making history. I thought I had sacrificed position for the sake of my family, but the wealth that previously eluded me was finally mine. I could retire early with more than a man could make in two lifetimes. Could life get any better? I had played my cards well and now I was being rewarded, or so I thought. Actually, I was being prepared for much larger challenges.

It started with two million dollars. "Mike," a WorldCom executive offered. "We'd like you to act as a transition officer and help integrate MFS with WorldCom." If I simply stayed on for one year as MFS and WorldCom merged, I would receive two million dollars worth of restricted stock. I didn't need the money. I was set for life, but I decided to take the offer anyway. I felt somewhat responsible for our former sales and support staff, and I liked the idea of making sure their voices were heard and that they were being treated fairly during the transition. From the beginning I knew it would be a stretch as WorldCom's headquarters were in Jackson, Mississippi, but by that time it was little expense to have a jet fly me back and forth.

For the protection of shareholder interests, MFS had negotiated seats on the new WorldCom board. After a few weeks of commuting, I knew what was really going on inside WorldCom, and it was ugly. On one particular day the Omaha-based board of directors flew down from Omaha to Jackson.

At dinner that night the atmosphere was ripe with arrogance, "Man, we are in the prime of our lives and it's just gonna get better! The stock will rise so high everything we touch will turn to gold." WorldCom's executives pompously guessed where the stock might go. They were drunk with ambitious pride, and laughed esoterically at their unashamed greed. They believed they would be the wealthiest men on the planet. Worst of all, they believed they *deserved* it.

Near the end of dinner, WorldCom's CFO, Scott Sullivan, pulled me aside, "At the board meeting tomorrow, I am going to present a document that says that, prior to the merger, twenty-plus million was approved for WorldCom's senior executives in the form of a bonus." He wanted the board to ratify a fake document even though it hadn't been approved.

The Securities and Exchange Commission dictated that everything, including revenues, expenses, and pending lawsuits, must be disclosed prior to sale since each could affect the value of the company. In our particular situation, I knew that we needed to have reported whenever executives would be compensated over one million dollars. They hadn't disclosed the twenty million in our "due diligence" documentation. Besides, what he was asking me to do was illegal.

One lie. That was it. I just had to show my support for a top executive by lying to Omaha's WorldCom board members. I shook my head in dismay, "You are asking me to deceive the Omaha board members."

"Mike, please!" he reacted sarcastically. "You and your other MFS buddies walked away with more money than you know what to do with. All I'm asking is that these executives get rewarded for how much work it will take to actually merge the companies together."

"I don't think I can do what you are asking me." One lie and I could keep the two million. Would I consider it? Nope, I couldn't.

His tone was vindictive, "Several of our executives won't stick around if we don't take this action!"

The board members aren't stupid. I thought. *If it wasn't in the minutes of the board meeting, or due diligence documentation prior to the merger, they'll know it's false.*

"At least sleep on it."

You can't rewrite history... I was frustrated. I knew exactly what I had to do, but I also knew that I would be letting go of the two million in stock. I needed to talk to the woman who had always been my greatest counsel, and as of late, the person with whom I could let my guard down. I just needed to hear her voice to know that I was sane and confirm that I was making the right decision.

Robbie was in the midst of realizing her deepest desires. We were living close to her family in Omaha and she had just birthed our third child and second boy, Christian. Together we had ventured out, leaving the pursuit of wealth behind to live a new life with family as priority and according to the core values with which we had been raised.

Now my character was being tested, "Rob, if we do this we will lose that stock…it's a lot of money."

Robbie's voice didn't falter. She was steady and strong, as always. She didn't just support me, but she also called my character into action, "I don't care about the money, Mike. You are not going to lie."

"Are we ready for the consequences of this decision?"

A resounding, "Yes."

It had been decided: I wasn't going to sell my integrity for money. It was late. 10:12 p.m., but I had to call the head of our board delegation and let him know. By the next morning, when the Chairman and CFO attempted to present the erroneous document, lawyers had already been called and we were prepared.

One of our board members stated, "This matter should have been disclosed by due diligence. If you do this, we will sue you," and it was over. I was out. The good news was that I wouldn't have to deal with WorldCom's politics much longer.

Sure enough, I received a phone call a few days later, "This isn't working out, Mike." What was not said, but certainly implied was, "Yeah, you can forget the two million!"

It wasn't the end, however. Over a month later I received a phone call from John Sidgmore, the former UUNET CEO and current WorldCom board member. "They've decided to honor your contract, Mike." John had fought for me to receive the two million, and I was ecstatic!

Wow. I thought to myself. *I really can trust you, God…if I just do the right thing.* There is justice, after all. Good can win in the end. I had read about Abraham's life in the Old Testament of the Bible. God had promised him that if he trusted and obeyed Him, He would bless him beyond measure. It felt like an easy plan: trust God and be rewarded. In my mind, I began spending the providential two million like a drunken sailor. If only I had realized then that trusting God doesn't necessarily mean that my life will go in the direction I want.

QUESTIONS FOR REFLECTION

1. Does your "walk" match your "talk?" When asked to compromise, will you stick to your values regardless of consequence?

2. Do you have counsel or truth-tellers in your life? Who are they?

CHAPTER 10

— New Challenge —

"God whispers to us in our pleasures,
speaks in our conscience,
but shouts in our pains:
it is His megaphone to rouse a deaf world."
C.S. LEWIS [14]

A LEXIS LOUISE FRANK," Robbie stated cheerfully, "That will be her name." It was two days before Thanksgiving, 1997. Just eighteen months after Christian was born, Robbie was about to give birth to our fourth child. It had been a while since she bought tiny girls' clothes and she was having fun.

At first I had not liked the idea of yet another child. Not only was Robbie forty-four years old, but our lives were demanding: Christian was a toddler, Robbie's mom was still in rehabilitation from the accident, and I was on another adventure in business, one that was culminating into the best venture yet. But it was Robbie's dream, and I wanted her to thrive.

She said to me innocently, "I told God that my body is His. If we are supposed to have more children, then it will happen!"

"But, you forgot to include me in that prayer!" I chided her. It made me nervous, but I was not about to refuse her. So, here I was standing at the foot of the hospital bed in the birthing room, expectantly waiting to see my little girl's head crown. Dr. Sjulin was next to me. Our girl hadn't come out on time, and because of Thanksgiving, she induced labor.

"Push, Robbie!"

Robbie strained and pushed. I was proud of my wife. She was so strong, even in her forties.

"Push again, Robbie!"

I would be the first to see her. I was excited!

Suddenly as I gazed at my baby daughter's face, I choked. *Wait a minute!* My heart felt like it had stopped beating.

Something is wrong! It was not what I expected. She looked broken. Her lip was split in the middle and the groove ran through her palate to the base of her nose. Her skin was a purple luster and even her ears seemed to be lower on her head than they should be. *Oh no! She looks dead…is she even breathing?*

Dr. Sjulin momentarily placed our little girl on Robbie's chest, and then hurriedly picked her up and ran for the intensive care unit. She gave no other explanation than, "She seems to have a problem…"

Robbie fluctuated between optimistic declarations, hoping that she merely had a cleft palate, and weeping, in case it was more serious. I felt like a knife had pierced my heart. *My baby girl…!*

I didn't understand. The ultrasounds had come back perfectly normal. At the last ultrasound the technician assured us that other than a slightly squished nose, she was a healthy eight-pound baby. Seeing my daughter in that condition shook my life paradigms. I was the guy who walked around in public completely oblivious to handicapped people. Never once had I wondered, *What is life like for them?* As sad as it sounds, they simply didn't exist in my world. Successful, well-educated, and non-handicapped people sur-rounded me. I was the guy who flew to work in a jet and played golf at the best country clubs. I hadn't made room for someone different than myself, particularly someone who could not function normally. *Broken doesn't fit in my world*, I couldn't help but think. *What am I going to do?* I felt betrayed by God, and I couldn't stop wondering, *Why?*

Everything I had ever trusted no longer mattered. It didn't matter that I had reached the pinnacle of the business world. In this case, making the right decisions had not equaled a good outcome. I began to question, *Maybe I'm not really in control of my life…Have I trusted You in vain, God?*

I was afraid.

"PLEASE, UNDERSTAND ME"

At 1:38 a.m. I was a captive pacing the insensitive, whitewashed hallways of the Neonatal Intensive Care Unit (NICU).

"Please, I just want a diagnosis," I had begged too many times already.

"Sorry, Mr. Frank." the nurses repeated in attempt to ease my mind. "We don't know what's going on yet. She's got quite a few things wrong…let's give it a day or two."

A day or two…will Lexie last that long? I wanted to know how to help her. I had to fix her pain. It was so difficult to simply…wait… while she suffered.

The on-call doctors came and went, most with coffee cups in

hand to aid them during their long shifts. They were merely night phantoms, appearing and then disappearing again. After several hours of watching them, I started to understand. They had seen my family's situation before, maybe countless times. Robbie and I were just another shipwreck in a sea of tragedies. The doctors knew how to stay afloat on tumultuous seas without looking back. They couldn't afford to. Nor could they stop and show compassion because then they would become captives like me. Tomorrow would only bring another tragedy, and the next day, another. They smiled and spoke what wisdom they could, "Mike and Robbie, live in the moment. Love Lexie and embrace her."

Hope was too painful, and I couldn't lie to myself—Lexie was on a respirator. She didn't just have a cleft palate. No one knew what had happened to her in the womb. The truth was that her predicament glared at me without resolve. It foretold that her prognosis would be complicated.

This was one situation I couldn't out-maneuver. I couldn't control the outcome, nor could I buy my way out of it. There was no way to win. I was thoroughly helpless, a captive trapped in hopelessness.

I told God multiple times, *I want my life back. Pain-free, and safe.* I couldn't handle the pain. *Don't leave me here among the weak and wounded, God. I don't want to be a victim.*

FLYING HIGH WITH LEVEL 3

The summer before Lexie's birth, just when I thought I had graduated from the corporate game, I was offered the greatest opportunity of my life. At that point, Lexie's birth was still several months away and although I knew our family would be financially well off for life, I was looking for a new business to expend my energy.

James Crowe, the past CEO of MFS invited me and three other former MFS executives to his house. "I want to make another play in the telecommunications arena. But this time, I want our play to be even better," James told us. Then he asked, "What are your ideas?"

We weighed our answers carefully, and decided that we wanted to build another telecommunications network. This time, however, it would be an end-to-end network not only for voice traffic, but also for data traffic (i.e. The Internet). That sounded easy enough. Those of us present could create an employee-centric culture, and hire like-minded executives and talent.

The next step was coming up with our business strategy. What would our play be? We believed that Internet expansion would include being able to move large amounts of data fast while still being cost efficient. We imagined building a network that was capable of carrying large volumes of Internet traffic around the world. At the time, Federal Express was the most efficient option for sending important data from one location to another in twenty-four hours, at a rate of twenty dollars. With new technology, we would send the same data instantaneously for pennies.

We knew this was a game-changer. Public demand for the Internet was increasing. Businesses, universities, and individuals wanted to surf the net and send data online. We could build the infrastructure including fiber optics, switches and routers that would allow major telecom service providers, Internet service providers, and large companies to transmit their data via our network. We knew that if we were the first to recruit talent and build the technology, we would lead the future of Internet development and make a fortune. The possibilities were endless, and our thought was, "Why not us?" That day with Jim Crowe marked the beginning of our most profitable business venture yet. We named our company Level 3 Communications after the backbone of the Internet protocol structure, which was known as the "third level."

From the start, Level 3 acted like a multi-billion dollar company. Financing wasn't an obstacle. James informed us that Kiewit Diversified Group, a private investment fund, would give us a portfolio of businesses and cash from their fund. We could do anything we wanted with the fund to create start-up capital. Within a short period of time, we had sold or spun off many of the assets from Kiewit Diversified and accumulated about four billion in cash. Not only that, but our idea was an easy sell. Who didn't want to transmit data instantly for considerably less money? We quickly raised an additional ten billion dollars from other investors. Normally as the head of Human Resources, I wouldn't have been included in the founder's stock awards, but I was given the option to buy into Level 3 at a very low cost basis and receive stock options.

After scouring the United States for the most favorable and attractive business climate to build our company, we settled on Boulder, Colorado for Level 3's new headquarters. The city was beautiful. It was the home of the University of Colorado, had an outdoor culture that our target recruits would like, and it was near enough to Denver that spouses could find work. It was perfect for the young "techies" we wanted to attract. We would no longer work with men we thought were assholes, men who were greedy and only cared for their own egos. We would hire talent that matched our core business values, and create an environment where that talent could thrive. My job was critical. I needed to recruit the best talent and allocate that talent immediately into new assignments. It was a daunting task, but I was grateful, excited and challenged. I was living among the kings of Omaha: legendary men who had accumulated significant wealth. It was the highest performance moment of my life. I had never been so fulfilled in business. Then, Lexie was born.

QUESTION FOR REFLECTION

1. When the storms of life come, what and whom will you hang on to?

CHAPTER 11

— Lexie's Story —

*"He that is on a lee shore,
and foresees a hurricane,
stands out to sea and encounters
a storm to avoid a shipwreck."*
CHARLES CALEB COLTON [15]

A NOTHER SHIPWRECK *in a sea of tragedy.* That's what we were.
It was one of the loneliest places I had ever been. Robbie's
happiness disappeared. She was exhausted and full of sorrow. I had
never been good at knowing how or what to do for her, and it was
only Day One at the NICU.

Days Two through Four became a dark blur of hopelessness. Lexie
underwent test after test without prognosis. "We'll let you know as
soon as we know something," we were told unceasingly.

Day Five became the allotted day that changed the course of
our lives forever. We were asked to meet with a panel that included
a neurologist, two geneticists and several nurses. Seated together
around a table, one of the geneticists cleared his throat and began
reluctantly, "This is an unusual case. Lexie has a strange mutation."

A mutation? Don't say it like that. She's not a creature…she's my baby girl.

"During Robbie's pregnancy, one of the strands of Lexie's 13th chromosome translocated to one of her 11th chromosome. It is a condition generally known as Trisomy 13. No one knows how this happens to a fetus, and it could even be a genetic defect. Her mutation is so rare that nothing on her particular condition has been published in medical journals."

Neither Robbie or I could say anything, but my mind prodded silently. *So what does that mean?*

"The translocation created countless internal and external problems. As you can see, she has a cleft lip and palate. Her ears are low set and have tiny pinprick holes. Her fingernails are flat and lack the patterns you would find in normal infants.

Please end my agony. Will she live?

"Mr. and Mrs. Frank," he paused before continuing, as if desiring us to prepare for the weight of his words, "We don't know what's going to happen to Lexie, and we think she is probably blind and deaf."

My mouth was dry, and my heart pounded anxiously as the neurologist and others jumped into the conversation, "According to Trisomy histories, we project that she may have a neurological dysfunction and a defective heart."

Blind. Deaf. A neurological dysfunction, and a defective heart. God, I can't bear to hear anymore.

"Our primary concern is to make sure Lexie has sufficient nourishment to sustain life. We don't know the extent of her gastrointestinal problems, but we will, eventually. For now, it may prove difficult to simply give her the necessary sustenance for life."

Could it get any worse? Dear Jesus…help! I held Robbie's hand tightly, knowing that it would be easier for us if we stayed connected. My eyes had been riveted on all of the speakers, but I quickly shot a glance at Robbie and saw silent tears spilling from her eyes.

There wasn't any time to process their words. The geneticist continued, plowing through his diagnosis, clearing the path for the end result. "Fetuses in this state rarely make it full-term. Eighty percent of Trisomy 13 infants don't survive past three months. In the cases we've identified, Trisomy 13 infants die from the complications of their condition. We don't know of any who have survived more than a year."

You mean you let death happen naturally? I still couldn't speak. *I can't watch my daughter die!*

Squeezing Robbie's hand, I looked over at her again. She seemed frozen in anger. *Oh God.* Attempting to do something, I uttered the words I had asked so many times before, feeling like someone else was speaking far away, "Can you give us a prognosis?"

"We wish we had one…but we don't. The good news is that Lexie has already beaten the odds."

My youngest daughter's life was hanging over a chasm of death. As if that wasn't enough, I had another problem. My role at Level 3 Communications was critical to its success, and our other three children needed us as much as Lexie. Amber had just begun college and was on the threshold of adulthood. Dustin was still in high school, but continuing to exert his independence against us. Christian was a toddler and required constant attention and supervision.

How am I going to handle all of this, God? I don't know what to do and I can't leave Robbie alone…

In the middle of that fifth night when I couldn't sleep, I visited

Lexie in the NICU. She slept silently and peacefully, as if there were nothing wrong.

Daddy's here, Lexie.

I looked down at her tiny frame, wishing I could pick her up and hold her, but she was separated from me by glass, locked away in an incubator and attached to a respirator. She was so close, yet so far. And there wasn't anything I could do to change the circumstances.

I want to hold you, Sweetheart. I want to touch your tiny toes and feel your little fingers cling to mine. I'm so sorry that this has happened to you...

I gazed at her affectionately. The nurses had placed a tiny pink bow on her head. Her full name was Alexis Louise Frank, but that night I named her "Kitten." I don't know why—it just sounded right.

Don't be afraid, Kitten. Daddy's going to make things all right.

The truth was that I didn't know how I could make things right. I was petrified.

THE BALANCING GAME

Level 3 Communications was on the verge of becoming the future of telecommunications. After six months of planning we raised the fourteen billion dollars necessary to build an Internet infrastructure across the United States and Europe. My job was to demonstrate that we could hire, inspire and retain the people we needed to succeed. We wouldn't receive any revenue until we'd hired the right talent, the system was installed, everything was running efficiently, and somebody made a sale. By the time Level 3 would be traded on NASDAQ, we would already be one of the largest telecommunications companies in the world.

"Mike, I can't imagine how painful this is for you," James Crowe spoke kindly after hearing the story of Lexie's condition. "We don't care if you sit out for a while. We can videoconference if needed. Whatever it takes, we want you on this team."

In the first few months of Lexie's life, it began to dawn on me that it was necessary to take the other executives' advice. I was forced to acknowledge that I couldn't be both present at home and operate at my optimum on the executive team. I knew James meant what he said, as did the others, but it was difficult to feel like I was the object of pity. We were professional colleagues, and thankfully we had also built a strong friendship. James and the others took on some of my responsibilities to support me. I was a founder and investor, and the company did not want to lose me. But it wasn't just about that. The executives at Level 3 genuinely cared about my family's well-being.

At some point I knew I might have to make the choice to leave, but I wanted to balance the distressing existence at home with my safe and predictable world at work. Level 3 was an escape from the foreign world of cold hospitals, dashed hopes and endless questioning. It was the only place I could feel safe, a world I could control. I understood who I was there and felt competent to succeed.

In Lexie's world, I was a helpless man. It was full of pain and I was weak. I didn't understand what was happening with my family. I couldn't escape from the emotion. I couldn't shut it off. The only option was to *feel*...and in the midst of feeling, I knew I was beginning to fall in love with Lexie. My carefully crafted image didn't feel so important now. All I knew was that I wanted to stop her from experiencing pain. I wanted to set her free.

I prayed: *God, why do I have to choose?*

THE CHOICE

Lexie stayed in the NICU two weeks. During that time she required a feeding tube, monitors, medicine, and even a supply of oxygen to survive. The nurses were a continuous presence around her glass box, working methodically to give her everything she needed. There wasn't much we could do but watch others care for her. Robbie and I ate at the hospital, and after the first few nights, drove home in the dark only to wake and repeat the cycle again. We would rest when we could. Our home became a sanctuary, a safe place where I could keep the possibility of death far away. Each time we entered the hospital, we resigned ourselves to God and prayed, "God, give us what we need today. Get us through, and please don't let her suffer." When we stepped past the glass windows into her world, we were required to "scrub in" and wear gowns. Her breathing tube would "ping" methodically. We could hold her, but she was connected to so many tubes that it was a difficult process. Nothing about Lexie's world was normal. I felt alone, like I had been abandoned by the person I had trusted most—God. I couldn't understand why my family had to experience such tragedy. Hadn't I done everything He asked?

At the end of the two weeks, Lexie's doctors called us into another meeting. "We are ready to release Lexie from the NICU and have you take her home."

What? You aren't going to take care of her?

"It is time for you to make arrangements for her care."

I was stunned. They had gotten straight to the point. We were on our own. Lexie had just gotten off the respirator. I couldn't understand why they would put us in this position. She still couldn't ingest food except through her nose. Robbie and I were amateurs, and if we didn't know what we were doing, I was afraid we would accidentally injure her. *You can't do this to us!* I screamed inside.

"I don't see how…" I began, but the look on the doctor's face told me there would be no debate. After that, I said little. Being responsible for Lexie's well being was not something I had ever planned on doing, and I felt paralyzed. No doubt our insurance company was pressuring the hospital to keep the cost of Lexie's condition as low as possible. I couldn't believe this was happening to our new and helpless girl. Twenty-four hours later, Robbie and I would be on our own.

Though we received little help from the doctors, the nurses were sympathetic to our predicament. That last day in the NICU, they prepared us as best as they could, showing us how to put the feeding tube down her nose, how to read the monitor, where to attach the cords, how to read and keep track of medication, and how to insert it into the feeding tube. They handed us a list of doctors: neurologists, audiologists, optometrists, and plastic surgeons. In one sitting, we were forced to learn what took medical professionals years. Feeling completely unprepared, we did the only thing we could do: protect our daughter as best as we could, and figure out everything else along the way. I could no longer escape from the threat of death. I had to face it head on, in the one place that had been my sanctuary away from reality, my home.

We transformed our dining room into Lexie's mini hospital, complete with a place for a caretaker to sit, rocking chair, medicine, monitor, and all other necessary equipment. I flew back and forth to work, but when I was home, Robbie and I shared shifts, fumbling our way through the feeding process and holding her while she cried. Robbie often slept on the floor next to her crib, and neither of us slept more than a few hours per night. Perhaps the greatest challenge was feeding Lexie. We had been told that in order for her to receive the most nourishment, she needed to be bottle-fed. But Lexie couldn't coordinate sucking, swallowing and breathing. She would gag and cry when we tried. The first time she sucked and swallowed successfully, we screamed in delight because it was a huge accomplishment for her. Often, however, we'd give up and resort to the feeding tube. Both Robbie and I would become angry trying to figure out the process. Lexie's wriggling body didn't help.

"Here, Mike. Hold her while I try and put the tube down her nose." I'd gently cradle Lexie in my arms while Robbie put the tube down Lexie's throat. Lexie would gag, scream and squirm during the process. It was frustrating to know that she was in pain, but I could not help her. It must have felt like a nightmare to her.

"Don't push too hard, Robbie, or you'll puncture something!" I'd warn in irritation.

Without medical training, we feared pushing the tube in too far and hurting Lexie. We also didn't know how to measure when she was full. Were we feeding her too little, or too much?

We'd repeat this process every three hours, sometimes without success. Every day brought new challenges and sometimes crises. I prayed continually, "God, don't let her suffer...please!" I blamed myself for her condition.

Without realizing it, we had abandoned our other three children. Christian felt the brunt of it. One day I heard Robbie remark, "If there is a hell for moms, this is it!" It was unbearable for her to go to bed while her two babies cried. Christian cried in his room because he missed us, and Lexie cried due to pain. Neither of us could comfort them. Christian would then crawl into our bedroom night after night. We'd snuggle him in between us, and try to sleep around his miniature form.

Robbie and I were fighting for survival just as much as Lexie, although it was in a different way. We were battling for our sanity, and...hope. The stress of caring for her quickly took its toll on our marriage. Rather than lovers, we felt like partners in a failing business, incessantly worrying and functioning as husband and wife only when necessary. We'd get angry and snap at each other, and then retreat to our separate spaces.

Robbie poured over the Bible, wrote in her journal and ran on the nature trail near our house. Out there alone with God, she wept. As for my personal reaction to the tragedy that surrounded me, I felt that my heart had been forced open. It seemed unbearable, but what I couldn't see was that I was learning to express emotion for the first time. Previous to Lexie, I didn't place much value on emotion. I had only begun to feel comfortable with the idea around the time of the Promise Keeper's conference. *Releasing* emotion was another level, I was beginning to be emancipated from the age-old adage, "Men don't cry."

I cannot say that I believe God intends to "break" us through devastating circumstances. Yet, day after day it felt like my strength and resilience were slowly being eaten away. The man I was becoming, a less confident and vulnerable "family man," was unrecognizable to the old me. In my estimation, I was losing my identity, but from an outside perspective, I was finally learning to let others affect my heart.

QUESTIONS FOR REFLECTION

1. How do you deal with stress?

2. Have you ever been "broken" by life? What did you learn from that experience?

CHAPTER 12

— Not Thriving —

"If you're going through hell, keep going."
WINSTON CHURCHILL [16]

L EXIE'S FIRST SURGERY was to stop the continuous vomiting after feeding. Surgeons performed a fundoplication surgery to strengthen the valve between the esophagus and stomach. A normally functioning flap prevents food from backing up into the esophagus. Lexie's flap did not operate properly, but after surgeons attempted to fix this, she became worse. Not only was she still throwing up, but her internal tissue was tearing every time she was sick. Their next effort was to insert a "button" into Lexie's side, which allowed a tube to feed directly into her stomach. A pump at the other end gently pushed nutrients into her. The surgery was successful, but her poor body could only handle a little food at a time, so it was necessary for her to be hooked to the pump eight hours per day. After the first few surgeries, our friends and family began to question our judgment.

"Why keep putting Lexie through this?" They'd ask.

Watching our baby girl suffer was excruciating. We had asked ourselves that same question numerous times, but something inside of us wouldn't give up on Lexie. Finally we realized, Lexie's life was not in our hands, and we would answer, "We will do our best to keep her alive until we know that it's time to let her go. Until then, it's not up to us to decide that she should live or die."

Thankfully, after the Visiting Nurses Association came to our home, they approved us to have a Licensed Practical Nurse (LPN). But as Lexie's condition worsened, Robbie and I stayed around her continually out of concern. Often, she would scream throughout the night. We'd get up even though we knew there wasn't anything we could do.

Lexie underwent many more surgeries. Every time, there was a strong possibility of death. We wanted her to live, and function normally without pain. Unfortunately, each time the surgeons attempted to fix a difficulty, they'd invariably discover new problems in her internal organs or endocrine system, and she'd undergo yet another surgery.

Robbie and I were continually treading water in a sea of bad news, but after watching Lexie push through every difficulty over the course of several months, we knew she was a fighter. However, we were not prepared when the people we had relied on most were no longer supportive. Lexie's heart had several holes and malfunctioning valves. Her cardiologist determined that she needed to have heart surgery, but the review committee at the hospital would not approve the surgery. Their faces were stone cold. They had probably initiated the same type of conversation uncountable times, but it felt as if they weren't even apologetic: "Mike and Robbie, we know that the situation with Lexie's heart is critical, but we must approve the surgery in advance, and at this point, we believe it is unethical for us to use the hospital's resources on a child that is not thriving."

The words "not thriving" were devastating. Couldn't they see that she had conquered so much already just by being alive? In the same conversation they asked us to sign a "Do Not Resuscitate" (DNR) form. I was livid, and walked away from the meeting wondering how the review committee slept at night after determining someone else's life wasn't worth saving. That night when we entered the front door of our home, we had to tell family and friends that Lexie would not make it. I felt so helpless. I couldn't control any circumstance in her life. There was no possibility but to let her rest in God's hands.

Besides wanting God to reach down and simply heal her, we still had one practical possibility left. A new pediatric heart surgeon had just arrived from Canada. He had been trained in the latest techniques and his work had been deemed miraculous. When we met with him, he was the first in the medical community to give us hope. He was confidently upbeat. After examining her, he said, "She is really feisty! In my opinion, I don't see why she can't do well in the next few years."

It felt like a nugget of hope. Robbie's countenance changed. I could see color in her cheeks, and faith in her eyes.

"I think I can help Lexie," he admitted to us with a smile. "Without this surgery, she will have a difficult time growing. But if the surgery goes well, then the time allotted to her on earth will be lived in a much better condition."

During the surgery, he found two other defects besides the initial problems he was trying to fix. Then, as we sat anxiously in the waiting room, an unfamiliar siren sounded, and I realized a tornado was headed our way!

"Everyone clear out!" an attendant shouted. The hospital staff immediately began their emergency evacuation plan. Robbie and I didn't know what to do. *What about Lexie?* There was no time to find someone who knew the answer. No one paid attention to our questions.

"Please everyone! Clear out!" We were herded into the parking garage below the hospital. Robbie and I sat against the cold cement walls of the garage weeping and shaking from fear. *Why now, God? Of all times for a tornado to hit!*

It was as if everything possible in the universe came against Lexie's life, yet she still survived! The hospital was more prepared than we realized. The Operating Room was in a safe area with backup power and did not need to be evacuated. The staff proceeded normally, and our dedicated surgeon was able to patch the holes in Lexie's heart.

For two days we waited in the family ICU, watching other families go through the same turmoil. Parents would walk in and out of their child's room, not knowing if their child would live until the next day, or even the next few hours. Many tears were shed as each family explained their child's scenario to extended family and friends. One thirteen-year-old boy had drowned. We were beside his parents when they made the decision to take him off the ventilator. We grieved with them, and understood their pain.

I wondered, *Will that happen to us?* We were on the edge of our seats waiting for either a miracle, or the worst that could happen...

After two days, Lexie crashed. Within a hospital, a Code Blue alarm is used to signify that a patient is "actively dying." As we walked toward Lexie's room, we heard the Code Blue alarm over the speaker system. Robbie began to shake from tears. Had our moment arrived? I wanted to cry, but my emotion was frozen in shock.

We continued to walk toward her room, tightly holding each other's hand and hoping that they had announced the wrong room. We anxiously looked past the nurse who appeared in the doorway to keep us from entering. Lexie's body was a pale blue color. They were trying to resuscitate her.

"Wait outside, please!" The nurse spoke sternly.

Just then a chaplain arrived to take us aside. I couldn't concentrate. I couldn't even pray. All the prayers for God to take her if she were going to suffer vanished. I couldn't lose her now! Not after living through the surgery and the tornado. Life could end so quickly. I needed to savor each moment. *Not now...not yet...*

Once again, a miracle occurred. Lexie pulled through! I will never know why she came back to us, but she did. I knew that this little girl with the crooked smile was melting the ice around my previously unfeeling heart.

FOOT TO THE FLOOR

Not too many days afterward, I gunned the accelerator. I was past the speed limit, but it didn't matter. My baby girl had stopped breathing...again. This was the fifth time I had raced along the freeway in my rental car towards the plane that would take me home to Omaha. I prayed that I would make it without being stopped by a patrol officer.

Lexie had experienced yet another grand mal seizure, caused by abnormal electrical activity throughout the brain. She would lose consciousness, have violent muscle contractions, and stop breathing. Each time, it was a life and death scenario. Her eyes would roll back into her sockets; her face would become purple in color, and her body, rigid. Robbie and I had never endured more frightening episodes. It was terrifying. But we had learned the power of prayer and surrender. The first time it happened, Robbie's friend who was visiting dropped to her knees to pray. Suddenly, Lexie gasped and was fine. Since then, during each occurrence, we'd pray, "God, if today is the day, then take her home. If not, then give her breath." Every time, Lexie would gasp and come back to us. Her story was miraculous to me, yet it never dulled the pain of watching her experience it over and over again.

Thirty minutes before, Robbie had called me in a panic at my office in Denver, "Lexie's had a seizure. You have to come home *now*."

Bolting from the office, I got in my car and called Robbie, "What's happening?"

"Lexie's not doing well," she stated, her tone fearful.

"I'm on my way! I'll be there!"

Suddenly, it sounded like I had lost connection. Then Robbie exhaled into the phone frantically, "She stopped breathing! I have to go!"

"Wait, Rob…!" but she had already hung up. The other end was silent. I redialed, hoping someone, anyone, would pick up the phone. It rang and rang without response. I swore to myself, and tried to keep my mind from imagining the tormenting picture of Lexie's body becoming rigid in Robbie's arms.

I illegally pulled over to the side of the freeway. I was shaking. *I can't do this anymore, but I have to be strong for Robbie….* I wouldn't know if Lexie had made it until I landed in Omaha, but I would never be able to live with myself if I wasn't there if she passed. I had to be there to kiss her little cheek one last time.

Something had to give. The longer I commuted back and forth between Omaha and Colorado for Level 3 Communications, the more it became clear that I couldn't continue to lead a double life. It wasn't fair to my family or Level 3. But I couldn't ask my family to move to Colorado during such a fragile time in Lexie's life. Her in-home and hospital care was routine enough that we had become dependent.

Lexie's condition wasn't the only reason why we needed to stay in Omaha. Due to her physical needs from the accident, Robbie's mother now lived in our basement, Christian was still a toddler, Dustin was slowly backing away from relationship with us, and Robbie and I were continuously fighting. I knew we would never leave each other, but I didn't know how we could repair the damage that was tearing us apart. We weren't functioning at our best, and because of that, I knew that Robbie needed the network of friends she had built in Omaha.

No, I can't make my family move during a time like this. Yet I knew I also wasn't performing well at Level 3. Instead of being an asset, I felt like I was holding my partners back. I hadn't slept well since Lexie was born, and my mind was drained, distracted, and not focusing well on the tasks at hand. A conclusion had slowly been forming in my mind. *I have to make a choice.* It was as if every situation pointed to the fact that my family needed me more than the company, but I was afraid to say the truth out loud.

The decision had nothing to do with finances. The stock I had purchased through my investment in Level 3 was performing well, and when we made a public offering, the stock doubled, and then quintupled. We had made more money than my family would ever need. I couldn't justify work as a means of providing for them. Rather, Level 3 was about my identity, my drive to be someone, and to participate in an adventure that helped me feel like a man. According to a New York Times' columnist, Thomas L. Friedman, in his book *The World is Flat*, the world has become flat because of ten major forces. Global communication entities like Level 3 Communications' fiber-optic network was listed among these ten, along with the fall of the Berlin Wall. Being a part of this team was a boost to my ego. We were changing the world! We drastically affected Europe, Asia, North America, Australia, and New Zealand. Soon after third world countries became wired when foreign nationals invested in our fiber optic cables. Globalization, Friedman writes, "made us all next-door neighbors." [17] How could I let go of my executive position on a team that was perhaps one of the most important of the twentieth Century?

James Crowe, Level 3's CEO had suggested, "Why don't you just take care of your family, but hang on with us as well? If Lexie stabilizes, you can always come back full-time."

And so, for a time, I lived in both worlds, but the thoughts that plagued my mind were, *Who will I be when and if Lexie dies? How can I let go of the success I have attained? Is that what being "courageous" means? Leaving all you've known behind to do something you know is right, but that frightens you?*

For most of my life I had negatively regarded people who were faced with difficulty, believing that they had gotten themselves into it. I was overly critical and bore little compassion. Now I was beginning to see things differently. That was what the possibility of death does. It parades the truth in front of you so that what is important can no longer be blurry. The truth, I found, was that I needed to let go of my extended life so that I could love Lexie...even if she wasn't around for much longer.

God, please let me make it home before my baby girl dies, I prayed as the journey home to Omaha felt unduly long and painful. I made it to the hospital in time that night, and when I held her little frame, staring down at her deep blue eyes, it felt as if she were saying to me, *It hurts, Daddy.*

I know…I'm here, Kitten. I'm here.

I had convinced Robbie to go home and rest. She was thoroughly exhausted. Not just physically exhausted, but emotionally, mentally and relationally.

God, what should I do? Am I being too emotional about Lexie's illness? I don't want to let my partners down…Give me a sign…

It didn't take long. I heard the Father speak to me in that instant. "Mike, take care of your family," and I knew that He was giving me the ability to choose. But would I choose family over work?

I was going to give up something I loved for someone I loved more. It was time for me to provide strength for my family…I finally knew the answer and I was at peace. I would leave Level 3 Communications and take care of my family.

Now I'll always be here, Kitten.

QUESTIONS FOR REFLECTION

1. What is your responsibility to your family? How are you fulfilling it?

2. Is your heart alive? How can you tell?

CHAPTER 13

— The Girl with the Pink Bow —

"Night-dreams trace on Memory's wall
Shadows of the thoughts of day,
And thy fortunes, as they fall,
The bias of the will betray."
RALPH WALDO EMERSON [18]

WHO WAS my little girl? Well, Lexie certainly had a unique and authentic personality that matched her pristine blue eyes, crooked smile, and endless laughter. After I left Level 3 Communications, I dedicated myself to her care, and I fell in love. For three years she struggled, many times teetering between death and life. It was always a gamble. I knew that any day could be her last, and somehow, the time spent with her felt sweeter because of that. At first, we had been told that she would be severely neurologically challenged, never functioning as a normal child, but she quickly disproved that assumption.

Despite the seizures, the retching and the continual pain, she'd smile and rattle the bars of her crib, jabbering away in her wordless language. She would make conversation with invisible friends often while riding in her car seat. Although she never articulated words, she knew how to communicate. Her personality was anything but weak, and the sparkle in her eyes and her presence seemed to command people's attention, as if she were saying, "Hey everyone, stop being so worried about me. I'm still here! Now...where's that toy I just had?"

Her cheeks would become instantly red in temper if I took her toy away, or if I did not do exactly what she desired. She'd figure out how to get out of her fenced-in kitchen play area time and again, or play with the doorstopper springs for hours, which would echo throughout the house, "Boy-oy-ing, boy-oy-ing!"

The first time I lifted her belly onto my head was the first time I heard her laugh, and she laughed so hard that she couldn't catch her breath. She lived within her own world of beauty. Often, I would cover her mouth with my hand and focus on her eyes. Her eyes would lock into my heart. That's how we would communicate. Then, she would grab my nose.

If people asked, "Does she talk?"

I'd respond, "She does through her eyes."

There was only one occasion in which she almost spoke. I was heading out the door one day, and repeated, "Bye, bye Lexie" several times. I opened, closed and waved my hand at her. Watching me, she opened and closed her little hand just like I had done. The whole family couldn't help but scream in excitement. "Oh my gosh! Did you see that?"

Lexie's appearance often made others feel uncomfortable, but she never cared or held it against anyone. In public, people would stare. Children were more apt to say something without inhibition, "What's wrong with her?" It broke my heart every time. At first it had been difficult for me to take her out in public. I felt stupid. I didn't know how to associate with the "poor and needy." But over time, I stopped caring what other people thought. I was falling in love. She was easy to love. Those that judged couldn't see what I saw. She loved me unconditionally. She didn't care about my flaws, or my "net worth." She was a daddy's girl, which I treasured, and I seemed to have a magic touch that brought her joy. We'd stare at each other nose to nose. It felt like she was saying, "Daddy, I love you so very much. Don't be sad. Everything is going to be all right." My little daughter, the one suffering through more pain than I could imagine, would comfort me, "I'm going to be okay, and I want you to be okay too."

It's ironic to me now that the most helpless person I've ever known changed lives by simply being herself in the midst of tragedy. She showed all of us that there was something cosmically bigger than what was going on inside of our perspective. As I would stare into her eyes, I felt Love staring back at me. My heart, which had only been half alive, opened up through her love in ways it never would have without her. It was as if she were on an assignment from Heaven to melt cold, broken hearts, and love them back to life.

LOVE STORY

Lexie's story of love was paralleled by another tale of loss. Her death was imminent, yet I wouldn't allow myself to grieve prematurely. I couldn't face it...not after I had fallen in love. No, I could not face her death, but Robbie let her feelings show. She held nothing back. She wept often and would ask for prayer from pastors, friends, and anyone who was willing.

In the beginning we had placed our hope in doctors and hospitals, and chased down every possible medical solution, believing that the answer was out there "somewhere." After three arduous years, we had learned to surrender her daily. The weight of responsibility fell to the ground. Robbie stopped pressuring the doctors, specialists and nurses for an answer. We weren't workers of miracles. We did everything we could to keep her comfortable and give her the best life possible with her condition. Yet, we were her parents, and not responsible for whether she lived or died. She was in God's hands, not ours. Most importantly, I began to believe that even if she died, God would not waste my tears or Lexie's suffering. There was a broader purpose at hand...although at the time, I could not grasp what that purpose was.

Despite our daily surrender, Robbie held on to the possibility of a miracle. Many "workers of miracles" had visited us since Lexie's birth. Their stories baffled me, and I—the left-brained unemotional man—was willing to believe that God could recreate her body so that she would be healthy. I did not care if others said we were foolish. She was my daughter, and I would do anything for her. But there came a point where I was so emotionally exhausted that I felt I couldn't pray anymore. I knew that if God didn't heal her, her life would soon be over. Not knowing what would happen caused me to feel that I was subjected to a continuous cycle of grief, and I wondered, *After all the prayers that we have prayed, why hasn't she gotten better?* I felt completely helpless. With a loved one's sudden death, you grieve, but eventually have closure. With Lexie's situation, I couldn't advance. I was in a constant state of unknown. I was haunted by the possibility of death every time I looked at her.

Some people live only in reality, others in fantasy. When Lexie was first born, we prepared for her death, not knowing what else to do. But when we understood that a miracle was possible, we believed in the impossible for the first time. Yet every time she was in the emergency room, the possibility of death returned to cast a shadow on our hope. I didn't know how to balance reality with the miraculous. It was very difficult to stand in the middle, but that's where I had to stay. When a miracle did not happen, I interpreted my unanswered prayers as God not loving or caring for my family, and I could not imagine *how* my family would ever become happy again.

When comforted by those who believed in God, I felt patronized. Their words didn't relate to the depth of pain I felt. I wanted God to come to me right where I was at, down in the darkness of pain, self-pity and loss. Hadn't I done everything right? At times I would become angry. *Maybe I missed something…maybe I am the one to blame…What "rule" have I missed, God? I thought You would rescue Lexie…?*

Amidst the questions about her life, I was also struggling with living outside of the corporate world. I was still young at forty-four, and I had expected the current years to be the best of my life. My work experience qualified me for the highest Human Resources' positions in the country, but I was growing less and less communicative at home. The years I had spent building my empire were gone. There was nothing left but the possibility of Lexie's death, which I was afraid would ruin me forever. Nighttime was filled with depression and despair. Although I never spoke the thought out loud, I imagined that God had swept away my dream life and placed me in a prison of sorrow. Would I ever believe in myself again? Everything I had so carefully built, trained to be, and fought to win was gone. I had become broken in a way that was unnatural. I wasn't at peace, and when I looked in the mirror, I felt old. I didn't recognize the guy with gray hair who looked fatigued.

"IT'S TIME"

My mouth was dry again. I wanted to say something...anything, but there was nothing to say. Once again I stuffed my emotion and listened to the surgeon.

"Mike and Robbie, I have decided not to do reconstructive surgery on Lexie's palette," Dr. Singhal said carefully.

Her lip and nose had been repaired, but in the last few months, an infection ripped apart the stitching. He continued, "When I considered the potential danger and the fact that she's not thriving, I could come to no other decision..."

The words "not thriving" continued to plague us. Dr. Singhal's refusal felt like betrayal. Didn't her uphill battle the past three years count for anything? They didn't know her like we did. She *was* thriving, full of life, challenging each problem as it arose with tenacity. But I knew the underlying issue, even if he fixed her lip and palette, was that she would never be able to eat normally. She still couldn't suck, swallow and breathe simultaneously. Eventually, the feeding tube wouldn't provide enough nourishment to sustain her life. He was not heartless—he was a realist. I was not. I wasn't willing to face the fact that, medically speaking, she wasn't going to get better. At least he was being honest face to face.

"I know this is extremely difficult, but I don't want to give you false hope." Lexie had defied the odds by living this long, but she wasn't becoming stronger. Dr. Singhal believed that it was pointless to subject her to more high-risk surgeries. He was informing us, "It's time." It was time to simply take her home and enjoy the days she had left. I looked over to gauge Robbie's reaction. Tears streamed down her face. I knew she wanted to explain to him, "But you don't know Lexie like we do!" Instead, she wept.

"You have done everything you could."

I wanted to resist his words, *God, is it really time for Lexie to go home?*

He had nothing more to say, "I am very sorry."

"We understand," I said the words, feeling everything inside shout in disagreement. Robbie and I got up and walked out of the hospital in silence, hand in hand. Tears ran down my face. A cool breeze greeted us outside. Thanksgiving would arrive soon. *God, how can I be thankful right now?*

When we pulled into our driveway, Christian, now four years old, came running outside to greet us. The red cape of his Superman outfit fanned out behind him in the wind. His presence, full of joy and anticipation, was exactly what we needed in that moment. Yes, I did have something to be thankful for. *I have a family—a wife, three healthy children, and for now, Lexie is still here...*

THE WORST PLACE IN THE WORLD

It was 2:00 a.m. Everyone else had gone to bed, and I held Lexie's body, covered in the sweat from physical torment, in my arms. I could do nothing but pray that she would fall to sleep. She did... eventually, but only after exhausting herself from tears.

Nights like tonight unleashed a chasm of emotion. She had stared at me with her clear blue eyes, as if she were telling me, "I am yours, Daddy. I am so happy you are my Dad."

I stared back at her. Her courage amazed me. She had just taken her first steps a few days before. *God, why does she have to suffer like this? Let me take her pain. Let me die in her place.* I had given my heart away to my blonde, wispy-haired girl. I knew fully that I would feel pain in the process, but it didn't matter. Pain had opened my eyes. Maybe this is what it meant to be a father. My world no longer revolved around me. At first I didn't want to touch the painful recesses of her life because it was foreign to me, but now I was starting to see the world differently. I had opened up my heart to bear the burden of someone else's suffering. I had learned to love someone who at first frightened me because I didn't understand her. In public, I had begun to notice the handicapped in wheel chairs. I wondered about their life stories and the stories of those who cared for them. I sympathized with the hurting. I *saw* them, saw through them and understood their pain.

I wondered if, previous to Lexie's birth, I had been so lost emotionally that Lexie's suffering was the only thing that could help me find my way again. Yet where had it taken me? Now, I was exhausted, lonely and desolate. As a result, I closed myself off again. I kept the emotion to myself, because I believed I needed to be strong for my family.

It was at this crucial hour that I took a life-transforming trip. I had a windfall of extra money, and had been looking for a place to give. I knew that God had a bigger plan for the money than my local church. Since I was a friend of Clive Calver, President of World Relief at the time, I decided to give it toward a world crisis. But I wanted to go and give it away myself. Clive asked me, "Do you want to go to the worst place in the world?"

"No, I'd rather go to the best." I said in confidence. But I knew in my heart that the answer was, "Yes." I couldn't escape what God would conceive in my heart through the worst place in the world at that time, Sierra Leone. For months, I had been wavering between allowing my heart to open, and insulating myself from the vulnerability and connection my family desired. I was in this broken place when I witnessed the suffering of a terrorized nation first hand. I was in this fragile condition when I was forced to refuse the young girl's request to rescue her baby from a nation at war. I could do nothing, regardless of money or position.

The irony was astounding—whereas my daughter, raised with as much love and protection as possible, might not live because of a weakening health condition, this young girl's healthy baby might not live because of a lack of protection. Seeing this mother's desperation helped unwrap my emotion from its cocoon. I was beginning to *feel*...to taste...and even to touch another's suffering, and I finally began to realize that I would be willing to take on another's pain. I'd never be the same.

QUESTIONS FOR REFLECTION

1. Have you ever chosen to "shut off" your emotions? What were the consequences?

2. If you haven't been able to feel emotion, and you know there is more, would you be willing to ask for help?

CHAPTER 14

— The Unknown —

"Absence and death are the same—
only that in death there is no suffering."
THEODORE ROOSEVELT [19]

A YEAR AFTER my trip to Sierra Leone, in the middle of a night blizzard in March, my mind was plagued with worry. Lexie's breathing was labored, and she had a fever that would not come down. Since Robbie had gone out for a little while, the nurse and I cared for her as she screamed in distress. This was worse than normal. I knew that my only choice was to take her to the Children's hospital. Although it was never a good idea to admit a child on a Sunday evening since the regular staff would be at home, it was a brand new high-tech facility, and I trusted that the medical team would know how to deal with severe cases like Lexie's. I bundled up her little body as best as I could, and drove through the eerie darkness. The flurries of snow descended all around, making the drive extremely slow and laborious.

The Intensive Care Team quickly found the source of her pain. "Lexie has a bacterial infection, which probably came in through her heart catheter line."

I felt the color drain from my face. We had been warned repeatedly about the dangers of bacterial infections. If it wasn't caught early enough, she could suffer fatal consequences.

"Mr. Frank, she is rapidly becoming toxic," the stand-in doctor stated, worry evident on his face. His words meant that the infection had spread. "We will put her on a high level of antibiotics and run an IV."

"Okay," I responded, already numb with the knowledge of how difficult it would be to insert an IV into Lexie. "Do what you have to do." *Here we go again*, I thought.

The soft, pliable texture of her tissue, the weakness of her circulation, and the fact that her veins moved when nurses tried to "stick her" with a needle, compounded to make inserting an IV extremely difficult. Robbie and I had often advised the hospital staff to call a NICU nurse before trying several times without success. They rarely listened, and we were forced to sit back and watch as they poked and prodded our little one. On one occasion when they couldn't locate a vein in her arm, they resorted to using a vein in her head.

I knew that we had previously avoided this possibility, but now we must face not only the worst-case scenario, but also its aftermath. Thankfully, Dr. Gary Lerner, the Lead Intensive Care doctor came to the hospital after he learned that Lexie had been admitted. He specialized in extremely complicated cases, and he had advised and comforted us multiple times. He was a compassionate and patient man who had not become calloused through the tragic scenarios of his patients. After he checked on Lexie, he sat down with me.

"Mike," he began. His face was serene as he spoke, "Lexie is not doing well. Her organs are in distress from the infection. If I may be honest with you, we've always worried about this level of infection occurring, and here we are. We'll know if the antibiotics are doing their job in a few hours."

The next two hours felt like days as I paced the halls of the hospital, and prayed for Robbie's safety as she navigated her way through the snowstorm toward the hospital. I had called and told her, "You need to come now." I held back my emotion on the phone, worrying about how she would respond. She was already fragile due to her mother's imminent death. Her mother had never fully recovered from the auto accident, and at that same moment was being cared for in a neighboring hospital.

I walked back into Lexie's Intensive Care room. She had defied the odds of survival her entire life. And now, our hearts had become so accustomed to her that we hoped it would go on this way forever. I loved her so much. Despite the countless times we had watched her body go limp and then gasp for breath and come back to life, this time felt different. I knew it might be the end, but I was not ready.

Her little sleeping body was lined with sweat. I couldn't take it. *God, please don't ask me to pray, "If it's Your time, then take her," because I can't do it anymore!* I knew that releasing her would allow her to be free from pain, yet I was afraid I would not survive emotionally if she died. I leaned close to Lexie's face and whispered to her, "I'm here, Kitten. Daddy loves you. Everything is going to be all right."

In a split second, Lexie's heart monitor began to screech, "Code Blue!" Immediately nurses ran into the room, followed by doctors. "Mr. Frank, you must leave now!" They called hurriedly to me.

I couldn't move.

"Please, go!" Then they shoved me out the door.

How could I say "Goodbye" to her as the Code Blue signal echoed shrilly in the background and doctors and assistants treated her as any other patient? I walked away slowly, and began to pace. *How will I tell Robbie when she arrives?* I imagined the elevator dinging and the doors opening with Robbie looking at me from a distance. She would be chilled from the snow as she walked through the cold corridors of the hospital.

I checked my watch. Only one minute had passed. I kept close by Lexie's door.

Another minute. How many times would I check my watch and it would read the same time?

More time passed, slinking by as if inconsiderate of those who waited.

Whatever the doctors were doing inside was taking too long.

Eventually Dr. Lerner wandered outside Lexie's door in effort to find me. I walked toward him, anxious, yet afraid of what he would say.

His face was ashen in color. As he spoke, he kept his eyes lowered, "Mike, Lexie has suffered a massive heart attack."

I stared at him, finding it difficult to breathe.

"We were able to help her heart beat again with a defibrillator, but her brain was deprived of oxygen for a few minutes. Given the situation, I don't know if she will make it through the night. I am so sorry, Mike."

Dr. Lerner left me in my grief. It's difficult for me to admit, but I had reached a point where I knew if I held on to Lexie, it was more about me than her. It was selfish. I had to let her go. She would be going home to a place that was free of pain and the confinements of her physical body. So, I began to ask God to take her. It felt unnatural. No parent should have to pray that prayer, but I knew her freedom superseded my desire for her presence.

In the distance I heard Robbie call to me, "Honey...what's going on?" Her voice was edged with worry. She walked hurriedly toward me.

I knew she was scared. How was I going to explain what had happened? I couldn't face her. When she stood next to me, I gently grasped her hand and said nothing.

"Tell me." Her deep eyes scoured mine intensely. Lexie had her clear blue eyes and wispy blonde hair. I could hardly look at her, but finally managed to relate what had happened.

Her simple response was, "We have to pray, Mike."

At that point, prayer was made up of hollow words—words that could not express the depth of despair I felt. I did not have the grace to pray. I knew that Lexie was gone. Robbie took the lead and prayed what I could not, "Lord, if this is it, take her home. If You choose to heal her, then I want her back, but completely healed."

Robbie and I sat down to wait...

THAT KNOWING SMILE

Lexie's vitals stabilized and revived over the next two days. Many of our friends gathered around us in support. As we prayed, her vital signs elevated. Robbie and I both rejoiced. *Maybe God is healing her!* When the lead doctor of the Intensive Care Unit found out that tests hadn't showed permanent damage, he admitted to us, "It looks like she is doing better, but that's not possible!" He was astounded that she hadn't passed away.

Despite her vital signs, Lexie was still unresponsive except that she continued to have seizures. We were all hopeful until the team ran the first brain scan. They found very little activity. Her brain had been damaged permanently. I couldn't believe she was gone. Her features looked the same. But I couldn't see her eyes, those piercing blue eyes that saw into me. Her personality, emotion, joy, and the smile that seemed to know my secret battle, had disappeared.

Dr. Lerner would not give up hope. "But this is Lexie," he said, "and we don't know where this is headed. We will keep her on the respirator and run the test again in a few days." He had come to know our daughter as we had. She had defied the odds so many times, and had caused even those who did not believe in miracles to believe in the impossible.

Yet, the next set of tests returned to us with the same results. It was evident that Lexie's survival was due to the respirator.

"You don't have to make a decision. You are going to know what's right." Dr. Lerner advised.

Robbie and I already knew our answer. "We believe it's time…"

We would need to say goodbye. We decided she would be taken off the respirator the following day. That night I didn't sleep well. My life before Lexie seemed so trivial now. Death had awakened my heart to the things in life that truly mattered. Tomorrow I would hold my baby girl in my arms, kiss her cheeks, tell her how much I loved her, and then whisper goodbye. Nothing else mattered, but sharing that last moment with her.

The following morning, I lived out the scene I had imagined in my mind the night before. The medical staff ran an EKG one last time, still no brain activity. Before they pulled the plug on the respirator, Robbie and I walked out of our beloved daughter's hospital room one last time, leaving her in their care.

Ten minutes passed.

Fifteen.

Twenty.

Eventually Dr. Lerner returned. An indescribable emotion was written on his face. "We took Lexie off the respirator, and she started breathing on her own," he said.

Robbie and I were stunned. She had conquered death yet again! I could not believe what I was hearing. As happy as I was that she was still alive, I didn't know if I could continue to handle the whiplash of circumstance that had plagued Lexie's life from Day One. How many times would I need to say goodbye? I didn't have closure, only chronic grief.

Dr. Lerner gave us direction in our emotional distress, "Why don't you two go home?"

Lexie was still breathing a few days later, and Dr. Lerner gave us his recommendation, "It makes sense for you to take Lexie home. She won't be in any pain with a morphine drip into her system, and she'll also receive nourishment from the IV."

He was right, and I felt comforted by his wisdom. It would only be a short time before her breathing would give out. She shouldn't spend her last days on earth in a sterile hospital room hooked to monitors, tubes and lines. It was time to take her home.

We shook Dr. Lerner's hand, and tearfully said goodbye to the entire medical staff. We bundled Lexie's limp body. This time, we would not call 911 if she stopped breathing. She would no longer be rescued.

I felt numb. I didn't know how to respond. I could only concentrate on being present in each moment, and caring for her physical needs. I couldn't run away. I couldn't hide.

God…my heart will never be mine again.

QUESTIONS FOR REFLECTION

1. Has it been difficult to get closure in certain circumstances?

2. What have you done to maintain peace?

CHAPTER 15

— The Yellow Dress —

"God pours life into death and death into life
without a drop being spilled."
UNKNOWN [20]

I SAT IN MY CAR outside the department store. I couldn't bear to go inside. I couldn't make any decisions about the coming days.

Robbie found a bright dress as yellow as the sun. It had a white collar. She wanted Lexie to wear something beautiful on her funeral day. She wanted Lexie to look pretty, and be remembered in that dress. She wanted Lexie's blond hair and light skin to stand out. Robbie held it together for our baby girl, but I didn't even know if I would be able to look at her. She was having continual seizures. All I could do was plead with God to end her suffering. When the nurses told us that Lexie's lungs were beginning to fill with liquid and that her breathing was becoming shallow, I knew that He was finally going to answer my prayer.

Robbie and I did little besides hold Lexie, make funeral arrangements, and welcome those who wished to visit and say goodbye to her. I wondered if she lingered in order to fulfill their wishes. It is strange to me that despite my sorrow in those dark days of tragedy, I experienced more peace than ever before. Its inexplicable stillness quieted our questions and soothed our hearts. I thought back to how fearful we had been in the beginning. We had been so frightened to simply take care of our helpless child, but over the course of three and a half years, we had grown strong and were no longer intimidated by the enormity of her trouble. And now, in the safety of our home, Lexie could say goodbye to the people who treasured her.

On the second day of April, Robbie and I decided to attend the funeral of a mother of Dustin and Amber's friends. We knew Lexie didn't have long, but we felt it necessary to go. One of our friends had given us a hymnal, and Robbie grabbed it on the way out the door. The drive would be long, and she knew we needed comfort. Once inside the car, Robbie opened the hymnal at the song, "It is Well with My Soul." We began to sing the hymn together, and later Robbie told me of the author's tragic history. I knew that if he could endure what he had and still praise God, we would be okay.

The man who penned the song was Horatio Spafford, a lawyer in Chicago during the middle of the nineteenth century. His heartbreak began in 1870 when his only son died of scarlet fever. In 1871, his family lost their sizable real estate investment in the great Chicago Fire. Attempting to avoid further disaster, Horatio decided to travel to England with his wife and four daughters. A last minute business development kept him in New York, while his wife Anna, and daughters Annie, Maggie, Bessie and Tanetta boarded the *Ville de Havre* to England.

Nine days later Horatio received a telegram from his wife, which stated, "Saved alone." The *Ville de Havre* had collided with an

English vessel. A witness later described Anna standing proudly, surrounded by her daughters aboard the deck of the ship while it sank. She passed out the moment her baby girl was violently ripped from her arms by the tide of water. While unconscious, a board from the remnants of the ship floated beneath Anna's body and lifted her above water. When she woke, she was filled with despair. Then she heard a voice say to her, "You were saved for a purpose."

Immediately after hearing of the disaster, Horatio sailed to England. He was overcome by misfortune, but on the journey, the captain called for him to come to the bridge of the ship. Then the captain told him, "I believe we are now passing the place where the *Ville de Havre* was wrecked." Desiring to release the depth of his emotion, Horatio returned to his cabin and penned the words to "It Is Well with My Soul." The words are as follows:

> When peace, like a river, attendeth my way,
> When sorrows like sea billows roll;
> Whatever my lot, Thou has taught me to say,
> It is well, it is well, with my soul.

> It is well, with my soul,
> It is well, it is well, with my soul.

> Though Satan should buffet, though trials should come,
> Let this blest assurance control,
> That Christ has regarded my helpless estate,
> And hath shed His own blood for my soul.

My sin, oh, the bliss of this glorious thought!
My sin, not in part but the whole,
Is nailed to the cross, and I bear it no more,
Praise the Lord, praise the Lord, O my soul!

For me, be it Christ, be it Christ hence to live:
If Jordan above me shall roll,
No pang shall be mine, for in death as in life
Thou wilt whisper Thy peace to my soul.

But, Lord, 'tis for Thee, for Thy coming we wait,
The sky, not the grave, is our goal;
Oh, trump of the angel! Oh, voice of the Lord!
Blessed hope, blessed rest of my soul!

And Lord, haste the day when my faith shall be sight,
The clouds be rolled back as a scroll;
The trump shall resound, and the Lord shall descend,
Even so, it is well with my soul. [21]

Robbie and I made a choice that day, "No matter what happens, we will praise You, God. Even in our deepest sorrow, we will praise You. We will take the days we have left and celebrate her life." Hearing Horatio Spafford's story and letting the words of his song minister to our souls affirmed our hearts. We knew that everyone was waiting for us at home. Would we curse God and turn our backs on Him, or would we take victory away from the enemy of our souls by proclaiming the truth? Could we trust God enough to let Lexie go? Sometimes death gets away with injustice if it's about the people who are left rather than the person taking the journey. I could not let that happen. We had wondered if God was true to His promises, and now we finally knew the answer. We were ready to say goodbye.

When we arrived home and walked through the front door, I immediately climbed the stairs to Lexie's room. Robbie stayed behind, knowing that it wouldn't be long. When I saw the look on the nurse's face, I knew it was the end. I picked up Lexie and held her close to my heart. Then I kissed her tiny head.

"Robbie," I called to her, "You need to come in here now."

But as Robbie mounted the steps to Lexie's room, her sister called and told her that her mother had been re-admitted to the hospital. Robbie entered the room with silent tears pouring down her cheeks. She sat down in the rocker and I placed Lexie in her arms. It was just Robbie, the nurse, and me. By that time, Christian was already asleep, and Amber and Dustin lived in a separate house. Lexie's breathing became slower and slower until, finally, she stopped breathing.

The house was still. No one moved. All was silent except for Robbie, who began to wail. Lexie was gone. Kitten, with the deep blue eyes, wispy blonde hair and crooked smile, was gone. For so long I had wondered how I would handle this moment. Surprisingly, instead of despair, I felt a profound sense of completion...of victory. The nightmare of her pain was over, and she was free from the confinement of her earthly body. Her life had not been in vain. Whereas I thought my family would be ruined by her death, I finally understood that we had championed. I had touched death, but it had not scared me. Heaven was Lexie's reward, and the fact that she was with her King was a magnificent reality to me. Our broken and helpless daughter, who had never uttered one distinct word in her life, had sung a song back into my heart and brought joy to countless others. That night was the beginning of Lexie's eternal life, and the beginning of a new chapter for our family.

Never again would I place financial gain above the emotional and spiritual health of my family. Never again would I fall into the trap of believing that position and status were greater than love. Never again would I allow my heart to become calloused and emotionless to fulfill a vow.

My little Kitten had brought me back to life.

QUESTION FOR REFLECTION

1. How have you responded to tragedy or sorrow?

CHAPTER 16

— True Masculinity —

"Who dares nothing, need hope for nothing."
JOHANN FRIEDRICH VON SCHILLER [22]

I WOKE UP exhausted and confused. *Where is everyone? Why is it so quiet?*

Then I remembered. *Lexie is gone.*

Pain stared me in the face; there was nothing I could do to avoid it. I had to deal with it or I wouldn't be able to move on. But how does one who has always been afraid of intimacy deal with pain?

I don't know.

I knew I had neglected my other children, Dustin, Amber and Christian during the many crises of Lexie's life. How could we possibly become a healthy family?

I don't know.

Then there was the resounding question, *What should I do for the rest of my life?*

I don't know.

There were too many questions I couldn't answer. They hounded me for months, but I still couldn't open up. I didn't know how. Early in my life, the Church had taught me that I couldn't be angry at God. He was the Maker of the universe, and I was simply a peon, a person bound to servitude to a master. How could my frustrations be valid?

Finally I realized the underlying reality—I was depressed. I needed help. It was difficult for me to admit. Nevertheless, I opened up to a friend and counselor named Gary. Gary was a Jew who believed that Jesus was the Messiah, the Son of God. He spoke truth and I was able to receive it from him because he was incredibly honest about his own life. I knew I could trust him.

During our first appointment, I rambled for some minutes, trying to put how I felt into words.

Gary was an empathetic listener, but when I was finished talking, he simply looked at me and asked, "Mike, are you mad at God?"

I thought, *What are you thinking, Gary? No one has the right to be mad at God!* I didn't know what to say in response. Gary noticed I had been caught off guard and continued.

"King David was a warrior, a worshipper and a ruler. Yet if you read the Psalms, you discover that David was honest with God about his frustration, pain and anger. He was vulnerable and raw before God, yet God still described him as someone who was 'after his heart.'"

I could be totally open with how I felt? I had never been given that freedom before.

"Buy a journal," he said. "Tell God how disappointed, mad and angry you are. Don't leave anything out. He's big enough to handle your thoughts and He will still love you, no matter what you say to Him."

Strangely, his idea felt good to me. I would try. At first it felt awkward. It had never felt normal, or even masculine for me to be vulnerable, and let out all my thoughts and questions before God. I did it anyway. *Where are You, God? Do you even care about what I've been going through?* I released the accusation, complaints, and anger at the sense of betrayal, but I was only scratching the scab of the wound. I wasn't digging down into the deeper wound in my soul.

FACING FEAR

Fear has a way of paralyzing us. That's how I felt about my self-image after Lexie was gone—paralyzed.

My feelings caused me to ask, *Am I still a man?*

Sometimes tragedy can annihilate our sense of direction and purpose. The confidence that used to be my "norm" had disappeared. I was exhausted, overwhelmed and anxious about the future. I felt like I had shrunken into a smaller man who was hesitant to take risk or be involved in aggressive or high-performance scenarios. I wondered if I were on an irreversible descent.

It was the summer of 2004, and I finally decided to address the fear. "Mike," Robbie said, "It doesn't have to be this way." She knew that if I went on a "wild" adventure, I would find the answers I needed. Somehow, conquering the wild meant conquering my fear. I wanted to find out: *Who is Mike post-tragedy? Will he be a man I can respect? Because he's not looking so great right now...*

I chose Glacier National Park, mostly because "wild" creatures, or more specifically, enormous man-eating grizzly bears inhabited it. If I was looking for adventure, this was it. Glacier Park was wild *and* dangerous, but I needed to prove I still had what it took to be a man. The only way I knew to answer that question was to conquer my worst fear.

On a lazy Sunday afternoon when I was young, my brothers and sisters had decided to have some fun with me. Disappearing, they left a trail of evidence leading into my grandfather's big, dark tool shed. One of them dressed up in a bearskin and as soon as I had entered into the darkness, the "bear" jumped out from the rafters. It wasn't long after that experience that I began to have nightmares about bears. When I married Robbie, she was surprised to find out that I wouldn't watch movies that had anything to do with bears. My brothers and sisters had scared me so badly that I had avoided anything associated since!

So, here I was, going into the wild with Gary and a guide for four days. As soon as we arrived to meet our guide, he informed us that the trail had been closed due to grizzlies, but was recently reopened.

I knew it. I thought.

Our guide hadn't given up. He talked with the park rangers and received permission for us to go. "Mike. Gary. Great news! They have opened the trail for us."

Uh-huh. "Great!" I replied instead.

"We'll probably be the only ones on it, which is even better," he reported enthusiastically.

You mean, except for the grizzly bears. A thousand pounds of untamed, easily surprised, carnivorous and endangered species! What had I gotten myself into?

As a counselor, and someone who shows a "softer" side at times, I thought Gary might be as anxious as me. Gary voiced my question, "What about the grizzlies?"

"Oh," our guide grunted. "We'll keep our distance and make noise."

Gary was persuaded, and laughed as he slapped me on the back. "You didn't tell me I'd need to have my affairs in order, Mike!"

Glad the guide has a can of bear spray! I convinced myself as I filled up my water bottle.

Two hours passed without event. Then Gary pointed to a dark patch on the trail. "What's this?" he asked, looking to our guide.

"Bear scat."

"Nice to know." He glared at me in humor.

I didn't tell him that other signs were evident as well. Grizzlies were the undeclared rulers of Glacier. There were fresh bear prints on the trail. The trees were scarred with claw marks, and the huckleberries, their favorite summer food, were ripe and plentiful.

As I trudged along the path, contemplating if I had gotten us into a ridiculous mess, I thought about my executive status. I believed that if I found the right business scenario, I would feel alive again. But every potential door had closed. Nothing had happened.

Why haven't you restored my position in the corporate world, God? I complained.

Mike, quit whining. I knew that voice. I decided to listen. *You are so focused on a narrow definition of yourself that you are missing the bigger picture. You are more than a left-brained businessman, son.*

I thought I knew myself better than God. *What are you talking about, God? I am a no-nonsense, high-performing business executive.*

I was wrong.

Mike. The voice continued. *There is much more that you have never explored, like the creative side I have given you.*

I scoffed in return. *Me? Creative?*

You have never tapped into it.

Well... You have a point. I acknowledged. All my energy had been spent on business. I hadn't given that part of me any recognition.

Then I realized that God has unlimited creativity. He is a master at it! Being in Glacier was the perfect example. The mountains, the springs gushing water, the vast sky, down to the smallest creature, were all an aspect of His creativity. He had invented laughter, singing, beauty and even sex!

God was telling me that I was created in His image, yet I hadn't valued those aspects of His nature in me. I had always viewed The Arts as frivolous. Being industrious and hard working was valued in my working class family as I grew up. Art didn't pay the bills. It was a luxury. Was He telling me that art was something to be prized? I remembered the words of the second President of the United States, John Adams, and realized the truth. As a signer of the Declaration of Independence, he stated in reference to our war with England, "People and nations are forged in the fires of adversity." [23] That "adversity" was to fulfill a divine purpose. He believed in fighting for the benefit of future generations so that they would have more freedom than past generations:

> I must study politics and war that my sons may
> have liberty to study mathematics and philosophy.
> My sons ought to study mathematics and philoso-
> phy, geography, natural history, naval architecture,
> navigation, commerce, and agriculture, in order
> to give their children a right to study painting,
> poetry, music, architecture, statuary, tapestry, and
> porcelain. [24]

Today we are the freest nation in the world with ample opportunity to follow any course of study. Art was not frivolous. It was something beautiful that was worth fighting for. *Okay,* I thought.

I'm starting to get the picture. Well, God. You're going to have to show me my creative side…It's been covered over with layers of "responsibility" and "have to's."

As night approached in Glacier, we set up camp alongside a beautiful lake. Gary and I pitched our tent, and after dinner and conversation by the fire, we crawled into our sleeping bags. I was still thinking about the revelations God had given me earlier.

Gary began to complain, "What's our guide doing out there without a tent? He's going to end up as a grizzly's dinner!"

Tired, I mumbled, "Like our tent is going to protect us."

Our conversation finally drifted off. The wild's symphony began and I lay listening to its quiet lull, hoping to fall asleep. Every stick and rock happened to be underneath *my* sleeping bag. It was going to be a few long nights out there in the wild.

Suddenly, I heard a loud "Kapplunck!"

"What was that?" I muttered, adrenaline already coursing through my veins.

"Something big!" Gary whispered back, immediately sitting up.

Oh no. I thought. *It's a thousand pounds of grizzly in the lake! It smelled us!* I was past an anxiety attack.

"Hey guys," our guide called discretely to us. "I'm going to get an ID on whatever made that noise."

Yeah. You go for it. I'm all for you.

Gary instantly transformed into Jeremiah Johnson, the legendary mountain man nicknamed, Liver-Eating Johnson, of the American West. "I think we should go with him, Mike." He started putting on his shoes.

Great. Now the real test comes. "Okay," I breathed. I didn't want to be labeled a chicken.

We crept forward and soon caught up with our guide.

"We're right behind you," Gary called to him lowly.

"Yeah, I heard you," he said over his shoulder. He used his head-lamp to search the lake for signs of movement.

I couldn't hear anything. My mind raced. *What's that old saying? "You don't have to outrun the bear, just the guy you are with."* I knew I could outrun Gary, but the guide? *Stop it, Mike!* I should have at least grabbed a stick. I had nothing to defend myself! How was I going to explain dying this way to Robbie? *Well, I guess I wouldn't be the one explaining.*

Suddenly, the guide found something. "Ha!" he chuckled in relief. "It's not a bear."

"What *is* it?" I asked, trying to calm my racing heart.

"Look over there. It's a moose!"

"A moose?" Gary sighed in relief.

All that for nothing. Boy, I sure acted like a chicken.

Through the dark, the shiny eyes of a large moose with immense antlers stared back at us.

"He won't be bothering us," our guide stated with confidence.

We got up from the ground and turned back toward our camp in silence. We were heroes having faced danger in the darkness. The silence only last for a minute. I cracked up in relief. Gary and our guide joined in.

"You scared?" I asked Gary.

"Naw. Not in the least," he lied. "You?"

We laughed even harder. Gary and I had acted like two terrified schoolgirls.

"Hope he doesn't step on our tent," I joked.

We cracked ourselves up again.

"Yeah, I was scared." Gary confessed.

"Me too!" I admitted, slapping him on the back.

We continued to laugh for quite a while. Then the significance of the event hit me—my fear had been far worse than the actual event. What appeared to be a "grizzly," a ferocious, man-eating creature, was actually a "moose." Fear can cloud our reality and make something feel more intimidating than it actually is. These perceived fears can keep us from doing what makes us feel alive. The truth was that the *unknown* in my life was holding me back, but by facing what seemed impossible, I was given the opportunity to move past my fear.

QUESTIONS FOR REFLECTION

1. Has fear played a role in keeping you stagnant?
2. What have you been afraid to face? What could help you face it?

CHAPTER 17

— Nothingness —

"The meaning of our lives is revealed through
experiences that at first seem at odds with each other—
moments we wish would never end and
moments we wish had never begun."
JOHN ELDREDGE [25]

I HAD LOOKED fear in the face, and won. But sometimes healing is a gradual process. Gary and I continued to meet, and during each session he was able to bring more of my questions and pain to the surface. He knew that I was still feeling a lot that I didn't know how to communicate. I felt abandoned, like God had simply left me there to deal with the pain of Lexie's death and its aftermath. I had done everything I knew to do: pray, read the Bible and believe, but there was a "nothingness" that stalked me like a shadow. I was alone and my prayers hadn't been answered.

Finally, still sensing the "nothingness," and not hearing anything from God, I asked Gary. "Where is God in all of this? Has He been with me the last few years? Is He with me now? Does he even... *care?*"

Gary didn't respond right away, but thought for a moment. Then he stood up and walked behind me to place his hands on my shoulders, much like a father would with a son. "May I pray for you, Mike?" he asked, knowing that giving me patronizing Christian answers like, "God will get you through, don't worry," was not going to ease my pain. I needed to hear from God directly, but for some reason, I hadn't been able to.

"Sure." I was desperate for anything. I just wanted the darkness to subside.

"Hmm." Gary said. "It might sound strange, Mike, but I believe that God gave me a word for you." Then he laughed, "If I'm not hearing this right, it might sound really stupid!"

"Don't worry, Gary. Just give me the word." *Anything, please!* I thought.

"The word is...Kitten."

Kitten.

The word hit my spirit. I began to sob uncontrollably. Unashamed tears came, tears that I had kept within myself for too long. My shoulders heaved with the weight of what he had said. There were only three people who knew that "Kitten" was my pet name for Lexie. Whereas one might have looked at Lexie and seen a young deformed girl, I couldn't see her brokenness. I only saw her beauty. Her light topaz eyes looked just like Robbie's. She had tiny dimples in her cheeks, and blonde curls around her ears.

Even though she couldn't tell me what was going on inside of her, we had a spirit-to-spirit connection, and her spirit streamed with laughter. Many times I would kiss her little head, and she would try to kiss me back. I loved her so much that I had given my heart away, even when I didn't know the outcome. I knew that she would die eventually, but I didn't let it stop me. It was the first time

I had allowed love to ruin me, to let another human being capture my heart without restriction and without fear of consequence. With Lexie, I lived in the moment. I stopped thinking about what I would receive and focused on what I could give. Since I had quit Level 3, I spent most of my waking hours with her. When I looked in her eyes, I'd tell her, "I am completely yours. I will do anything for you because I am captured by you. I would give my life for you, Lexie."

The word "Kitten" didn't have to be interpreted. I knew exactly what God was saying to me. Instead of Lexie being the broken person, *I* was...*I* was broken and helpless. Just as Lexie couldn't do anything to earn my love, I couldn't do anything to earn God's. She never had to perform for my love, and I didn't have to perform for His. Just as I would have laid down my life for Lexie, God had already laid down His for mine. I needn't do anything. In as much as I loved Lexie, God loved me. But His love held an even greater capacity than I could imagine.

With one word, I was a changed man...*again*. I knew I could trust God. I didn't have to doubt anymore. My questions were answered. He cared. He knew *everything*. I could say anything to Him. The heavy weight of depression lifted off me. I didn't need to be self-protective anymore. I finally understand what true love was, and that I'd always experienced it and always would. Through Lexie, I had became a father with unconditional love like God was a Father to me.

Now, it was as if God was asking me, "Will you love yourself unconditionally as I have loved you? Will you love your family that way?"

For the first time in a long time, I anticipated my family's future. I surrendered to hope.

LEGACY

As you already know, when Amber and Dustin were young children I was off conquering the business world. Now, after navigating through heartbreak and facing the fear of the unknown, I desired relational success. I was a ruined man, and by being ruined, I was beginning to understand my role as a father. I wanted to pour out my heart with Amber, Dustin and Christian, as I had done with Lexie. I knew that if I continued to hold on to God's promise of love for me, I could give them unconditional love. If I wanted to be a real father to my children, I wouldn't just provide for them financially—I would set them up for success in every aspect of their lives. The only way to do that was to build relationship so that they never doubted my love. I wanted them to *know* love and to believe that they could do anything because they were loved. I didn't want them to feel the disappointment I had felt when my father told me I was "outside" the circle of men. That pain had driven my life.

When I thought about what I could do to change my failed relationship with my oldest son Dustin, I thought of legacy. What would I be leaving behind? Obviously, if he ever encountered financial hardship, he wouldn't suffer. But my children also needed me to provide emotional support, and Dustin, above the others, needed my support the most. His heritage as a son had been stolen from him by my misplaced priorities.

Dustin hadn't been an ordinary boy. He lived within the recesses of his imagination, and would often comment on conversation in such a profound way that we would be caught off guard. His talent in music was beyond other boys his age, and his creativity gave him opportunity in the same way that my vow to become wealthy had empowered me. Yet, he was often misunderstood in his brilliance.

He was categorized as a "gifted child," which made him feel even more insecure and boxed in.

Because his personality and gifting were completely different than mine, I had not understood him. There were moments when I tried to connect with him through activities like basketball, but as soon as he felt the competitiveness of others or me, he would shut down. I would become frustrated and give up. He rejected all that I had valued earlier on in my life: hard work, ambition and wealth. Although he was exceptionally gifted, he had no desire to follow my route by going to college.

"Why should I go?" He would say. "If I do, I'll end up like you."

His words wounded me and I let them build up a wall of offense between us. In my mind, the only way he could be successful in life was to follow my example. I was painfully wrong. For a long time I never showed affection or emotion. I thought to myself, *How could I possibly relate to his emotions?* I remember specific negative comments I said, trying to knock sense into him. "If you don't shape up, you're going to end up…" I hadn't been able to value him—I only wanted to change him. I tried to force him into the image I thought he should be...*me*.

Without realizing it, I repeated the damage my father had caused me, and recognizing that mistake made me nauseous. As his teenage years came and went, our relationship became strained, and I felt that my son was a stranger to me. I felt guilty and ashamed, *God, how can I possibly make up for lost time?* Dustin needed me, yet I had been absent. I didn't know how to reconcile the years I had been preoccupied.

One of my first attempts was to take him backpacking in Zion National Park, Utah. By this time Dustin was married, but he was having trouble. He believed that he shouldn't conform to societal norms because he'd lose his unique identity as a creative person. Like many artists, he wanted to live from his heart. He'd do random things like stay up all night, simply because he could, and he didn't want anyone to pressure him into living differently. So, I planned the trip with much purpose in mind. I stood on the premise that God had forgiven me for my mistakes with Dustin, and with time, Dustin would forgive me.

THE TREK

That night I began to understand. Before setting up camp on our third night, Dustin called to me, "Dad, forget about setting up camp. Come watch this."

It was natural for me to be Dad: take precaution, unpack the backpacks, set up camp before dark, make sure the fire was lit, and prepare for dinner, all for the sake of not getting caught unaware by nature's unpredictable dangers. I was always overly prepared and efficient. Now my son was asking me to enter his world, a world that was spontaneously creative rather than requiring a calculated agenda. He was asking me to prioritize relationship above efficiency.

We had taken a treacherous path through a narrow canyon. Its entrance had been marked by warnings of mountain lions, and its sides were formed of jagged rock. There wasn't an escape route, but we needed to take that risk to make it to the desired location, a plateau overlooking the canyons and peaks of Zion National Park. We finally stopped for the night near the plateau's 1800-foot ledge. There we were graced with a panoramic view of the park just as the sun began to set.

When I heard Dustin's request, I stopped being my typical self and sat down beside him on an overhang of the ledge. Our feet dangled before us and the wind blew so strongly that it made our position precarious. Yet, it was exactly what I needed—risk for the sake of relationship with my son. On the plateau that night, I entered his world for the first time. Dustin sat fascinated by the streams of red and yellow in the sky. He picked up a stick and peeled its bark. Then he threw the pieces over the ledge and we watched them take flight, twirling and dancing in the air. I was beginning to understand...

"Dad, I really don't know what to do next."

The moment had arrived. After days of exploration together, and countless moments of conversation where I had repeated, "Son, I am sorry," Dustin was finally opening up. He was choosing to be vulnerable because he trusted that my apologies were genuine. He needed me and I needed him. My son had returned, and I was overjoyed!

"I understand, Dustin. It's natural to feel that way. I was scared and confused at your age too."

Dustin was surprised. He turned his gaze toward me, thankful to hear that he wasn't the only male on the planet that hadn't figured out life. "You were?"

"Sure. We all make mistakes. Fortunately, we can persevere and learn from them." I was reassuring my son that he was included in the "circle of men." Although he had made unwise choices, he hadn't *failed*. Often, our lack of competence in life or relationships can make us feel that we have failed, when in fact we have simply *learned*. "Having what it takes" has nothing to do with "having it all together." It is braver to face difficult circumstances (even if we have caused them) and choose to walk right through the middle of them than it is to escape. *Learning* means we engage in the battle instead of being sidelined by disappointment. Real courage is not marked by always being right, but by *how* we deal with our so-called failures.

QUESTIONS FOR REFLECTION

1. What do you want to leave as a legacy when you die? Is "legacy" merely monetary inheritance or something greater?

2. Do you have a broken relationship with someone you love? What do you need to do to restore relationship with this person?

CHAPTER 18

— The Battle —

"For what shall we do when we wake one day
to find we have lost touch with our heart
and with it the very refuge where God's presence resides?"
JOHN ELDREDGE [26]

DURING OUR DAYS in Zion National Park, Dustin and I were out of cell-phone range and only encountered one couple who warned us to look out for mountain lions. The danger didn't bother me. I intentionally brought us into danger because it was my responsibility to show Dustin how to live in risk. I was just beginning to learn that risk didn't always look like climbing a treacherous mountain or saving a damsel in distress. It could look like opening up and sharing what we feel inside. It could look like...choosing to love. Through our time together, not only did I want to restore my relationship with him, but also show him how to apply what we were experiencing to everyday life.

Through my experience as an executive, I realized that just as my father had hurt me, and Dustin was hurt by me, more than ninety percent of men have received similar wounds from fathers or leaders. Some of us have never heard the words, "Son, I'm proud of you," or "You're doing a great job." Instead, we surmised that we did not meet the unsaid standard. Often wounds occur in seemingly insignificant moments, and the person inflicting the wound is completely unaware. Our dad, coach or even teacher says a derogatory comment and we instantly feel demoted from manhood to boyhood. We start to think that we don't have what it takes to be a man. We may either disengage with life and stop taking risk, or we may attempt to overcome our perceived failure by trying to prove our worth to the world.

Sometimes it helps, as wounded men, to face physical danger and conquer it. But we also need to face the man in the mirror. We have to be able to look at ourselves and answer the questions that we don't dare ask, like: *Do I have what it takes to be a real man? Have I locked away my emotion because of wounding? What do I need to do to unlock it?*

We must take the risk, face the danger of emotion, and conquer our fears through truth. The truth is that we have everything we need. Facing our doubt about ourselves is integral to becoming a man. We won't feel complete or that we "have what it takes" until we do. As Ralph Waldo Emerson, one of America's greatest poets stated, "He who is not everyday conquering some fear has not learned the secret of life." [27]

Essentially through my advice to Dustin, I was suggesting that in order to become a man, he needed to be both lamb and lion: vulnerable enough to open up and be in touch with his emotions, yet strong enough to face his fears and overcome them. In a series of poems called *Songs of Innocence and of Experience*, the eighteenth century poet William Blake, describes the paradoxical image of

God, as both lamb and tiger. [28] He presents God as mysterious and powerful through the first lines of his poem, "The Tyger."

> Tyger, Tyger, burning bright,
> In the forests of the night:
> What immortal hand or eye,
> Could frame thy fearful symmetry? [29]

The "tyger" is fearful, and Blake asks who could have possibly formed its mysterious "sinews"? He implies that the "tyger" displays the image of God's unfathomable strength. In his opposing poem, "The Lamb," Blake portrays God's vulnerable side:

> For he calls himself a Lamb:
> He is meek & he is mild,
> He became a little child: [30]

Just as Blake suggests, a perfect image of masculinity is found in the paradoxical image of both tiger and lamb. In Asia, tigers are known as the king of beasts. They symbolize royalty, fearlessness and wrath. If challenged, they are lethal. They are strong leaders, and although territorial, male tigers will allow the females and cubs to feed on a kill first. In the same way, men are designed to lead, provide and protect. Man has a need to be challenged and to conquer that challenge. Adventure is a naturally born trait. God wants to provide this adventure for us and take us on a wild ride!

On the other hand, one of nature's most vulnerable creatures is the lamb. As a lamb, God is merciful, quiet and emotive. The tiger is ferocious in defense of his territory; a lamb is innocent with a "tender voice." A man must also embrace emotion. The only way we will fully engage in the thrill of adventure is if we allow our hearts to be open. Why is it necessary to be both? We were designed in the image of God. It is often easier for men to display their tiger-like side, but not show compassion or vulnerability. Men have been told that vulnerability or emotions make them weak, but a real man is able to display his strength through his *lack of fear for emotion*. A leader in my life stated once, "Never be too far from tears, for it shows you are alive." [31]

Most of my life, I felt the need to prove I still had the ability to "be a man." After Lexie's death, I began to question what that meant. During my sessions with Gary I was propelled to embrace the misunderstood emotion I had locked away for years. I had been hiding. I had been the tiger, but I didn't know how to be the lamb. Releasing my pent-up emotion allowed me to answer the questions of my identity. I learned that I had always been loved, even in weakness, and that I would always be loved. Walking in the confidence that I was loved and accepted allowed me to love and accept my son.

QUESTIONS FOR REFLECTION

1. What qualities should a "real man" possess?
2. How does your acceptance of yourself affect your acceptance of others?

CHAPTER 19

— Finding My Magnetic North —

"Do not go where the path may lead,
go instead where there is no path
and leave a trail."
RALPH WALDO EMERSON [32]

LITTLE BY LITTLE, I learned to love myself. But during that time, I couldn't help but ask, *Where do I go from here?* So, I attended a Wild at Heart conference in Colorado Springs, Colorado. John Eldredge, a man who has written several books that have transformed men's lives in the Church world, hosts the conferences. I thought, "Why don't I just go to the expert? I could use a little heart surgery." From what I had read, it sounded like he really knew how to balance the paradoxical image in the Bible of God as both lion and lamb.

Whereas the Church has long asked men to be "nice and tidy" and fit into a tightly structured mold, John gave men permission to be free. He had no qualms stating that the Church has emasculated men, and that for men to be fulfilled, they need to explore the "wild" recesses of their hearts. John told us, "You are made in the masculine image of God—the image a warrior, not some passive, Mr. Nice Guy. Inside, you long for a battle to fight, an adventure to live, and a beauty to rescue."

So, there I was, listening to John Eldredge, hoping to hear something that would point me in a new direction, something that could tell me how I could meld my talent in the business world and the heart that had been broken by love. I knew that Bill Gates, Microsoft's CEO-turned-philanthropist, arrived at a point where he realized that he had to stop working for himself. It was after that point that he used his intellect, influence and financial resources to not only serve his employees, but also go on a journey to educate the world.

Finally, the challenge came. "Look back on your life," John said, "and write down the jobs you have held. Then ask yourself, 'What have I naturally gravitated toward?'" He continued, "It might be a deep-seated desire, so ask yourself, 'What desires has God put on my heart?' He has given you clues along your life journey, so go out alone, talk to God and ask Him to give you the rest of the picture. He will speak to you."

I was ready, desperate to hear what God would say to me. Outside the conference hall, the sun shone brightly, and I glanced up at the rocky mountains all around. *That's where I want to be*, I thought. *In the sunshine on that mountain with open space.* I hiked up a nearby hill, and sat down on a rock that overlooked the valley below.

"God. Tell me." I said out loud. "I want You to tell me who I am."

As I basked in the sun, I immediately began to feel an unexplainable warmth inside my body. Then in my mind I heard the words, *Mike, you are a guide.*

At first His response confused me. My definition of a guide was someone who led fishing, hunting, and backpacking expeditions into the wilderness. Although I love the outdoors, I didn't understand what He meant. As I began to contemplate other tasks of guides, I realized that they listen to others, and then out of their experience and talent, lead them to new places, places they can't find on their own.

It started to make sense. I had risen fast and reached an eight-figure income in the corporate world at a young age. I knew what it was like to be "in the club," along with its pressures, temptations, and sacrifices. It was difficult to remain in that scenario without compromise in one area or another, either sacrificing family for position, pursuing money, or even burn out. The greater an executive's power, the greater the temptation. I had attained the necessary experience to guide aggressive young executives along a path that would not only help them succeed in the corporate world, but also grant them the ability to look past themselves and create meaning in their lives.

"Wow," I thought. "I get it. I've been on their turf. I know what it's like and how to navigate through, especially when faced with tragic circumstances like Lexie's death." I could see how other men in the corporate world would need my help to guide them through the pitfalls. I could listen to them, challenge them, maybe even help realign their lives and then lead them into the *more* we all hope to find at some point in our lives.

It was as if God said to me, "See, I trust you now. Before such experiences as Sierra Leone, Lexie, and starting to rebuild relationship with your children, you were self-focused. Now you are a father to Amber, Dustin, Christian, and other young men and women who are in the same battle of identity."

My thoughts filtered back through the things I had recently focused on: the moment in Sierra Leone when the young girl placed her baby in my arms, my own baby girl Lexie, and my time with Dustin in Zion National Park. My heart had changed through those experiences.

"I trust you...you are ready," God seemed to tell me.

"I am ready," I repeated to myself. I couldn't help the excitement. Only God could have shown me how my corporate experience together with my broken heart over Lexie could benefit others.

"But," I questioned, "Guides are only in people's lives for a moment. It could get lonely."

"Mike, haven't I always been with you?"

"Yes," I admitted.

"Then, I want you to comfort others with the comfort I've given you. Become a father to them?"

The thought felt...right. This was it! Everything in my life, little and large, had prepared me. Based on my life experience, I would be a guide.

GETTING FROM A TO B

Essentially, my job as a guide is to "assess" others' life journeys. Sometimes, I tell them things they do not want to hear so that they can find a new and more prosperous direction. It wasn't always easy, but I knew that since I had changed the direction of my own life for the sake of family, I could help them succeed as well.

I am guilty of not responding well to people who have attempted to assess me along my journey, but it is a necessary component to reaching our full potential. I learned this lesson through a humbling experience. When Christian was eleven years old, I took him on a trip to Yosemite National Park. I hired a guide, and this twenty-something young man was the one who opened my eyes to my own need for external assessment.

"Okay, unload your packs," the guide told Christian and me. It was the morning of the first day of our trip, and we were ready to get on the trail, but our guide had a few tasks in mind first.

Christian moaned. I had already made him pack and then repack his backpack several times. As a junior high kid, he just wanted to get to the exciting part of the trip. He didn't care about the tedious details.

I sighed conspicuously, but obliged the guide's request. I stared at his long hair tied back by a red bandana. He was making faces in reaction to the contents of our backpacks. I thought to myself, *I've done this more times than you have.*

The guide frowned, "Why do you have all these extra clothes? You can wear the same pants several days." He continued, "Summer sausage? Chocolate bars? Those won't provide you with the energy you need for a grueling trip like this."

I folded my arms. I was becoming angry. *Just who do you think you are?*

"Cream cheese? Are you kidding me? What are you going to do with that?"

You know what? All I want are a few creature comforts, so back off! I said to myself.

Now Christian was smirking. He thought this was funny. His dad was usually giving orders to others. He hadn't seen me be directed like this before, especially not by a young self-confident nature-lover. I was not happy.

The guide didn't seem to care that I was upset. He simply looked at me and stated, "Mr. Frank. If you take all this, you will only end up carrying a lot of unnecessary weight. These extra pounds will weigh you down and deplete your energy."

I got it. He was assessing my preparedness and found me lacking. That was humbling, especially coming from a young man with half of my life experience. But, it was necessary. Assessment requires that we go beyond looking in the mirror, and include others in the journey. We can't assess ourselves and be on target. If we don't allow people to give us feedback, we will never see the full picture. Most of us ask our spouses, parents and friends. This is often helpful. However, we need to be open to receive assessment from those outside our family and friend circle as well. They should have an opportunity to evaluate our journey and give us an honest, and sometimes challenging review.

QUESTIONS FOR REFLECTION

1. Find out if you are operating in "burn-out" mode by asking yourself the following question: "When is the last time you experienced joy or enjoyed dreaming?"

2. Do you believe that you could enjoy life more? What is the next step?

CHAPTER 20

— Help from a Friend —

"Choices are the hinges of destiny."
PYTHAGORAS [33]

S OMETIMES IN LIFE, we miss the Cairns, the trail markers that are supposed to guide us to our destination. We might have started off feeling alive, knowing exactly where we were going. Everything was running smoothly. We were confident, thinking, *This is what success feels like!* Then suddenly, we are hiking a trail that is taking us in a different direction, a direction we didn't plan on going, and our confidence is left behind. Until Lexie came along, I had followed Cairns that led me to the greatest moneymaking and thrill-seeking adventure of my life. Then, suddenly, my confidence was torn away, layer by layer.

Some of us hide behind the mask of, "Everything is fine," but inside we are scared to death that we've missed it. We are no longer in safe territory and we are taking risks we can't afford. The vision that we once had is forgotten, as business becomes a scramble to make ends meet. We are eventually worn down to the lowest point of human existence—survival. If we are smart, we will admit that we are lost. If we don't, our lack of assessment will eventually kill us. It is difficult to admit that things aren't working, but that is exactly what is required to propel us out of survival mode. Being open, honest and vulnerable is courageous, and with courage, we can take risks that would normally frighten us.

This was the status of a man named Brett when he came to me for counsel. Brett was a fiery young man with an enthusiastic countenance. Those around him benefited from his fatherly nature, and his sense of humor (like wearing hot pink bow ties) and gave him a unique edge. Brett had everything going for him. He had a beautiful wife, children, and he and his business partner had started a marketing company from the ground up in Santa Barbara, California. They were successful and had built many profitable business relationships in the community. He was well known and respected, but when he came to me, his honest admission was, "I just don't have it in me to be brilliant for people any more. I am tired of being the 'idea guy' who provides answers."

A common occurrence with creative geniuses is that clients merely suggest a notion of what they want, and rely on the "creative" to fill in the rest. It was obvious to me that Brett was burnt out. He had lost his sense of purpose and motivation. Life wasn't exciting or challenging, and he certainly didn't feel like he was living in adventure anymore.

"I don't know what to do," he continued, "Shouldn't I feel better about my life? If I have reached my 'destiny,' wouldn't I have a huge agency already?"

It was time for Brett to be open to an honest assessment. He'd have to be humble. Regrouping, drawing back, or shutting down a business could be painful, especially when his employees depend on him for livelihood.

"Well," I said, encouraged that Brett was being real with me. "Let's walk through possible scenarios: you could keep the company while building another source of income; you could sell it; or you could shut it down." We discussed these options for some time, and then I finally told him the cold and undeniable truth, "It sounds like you need to let your dream die."

He looked at me in shock, "After all this time? After all the energy and sacrifices I have made?"

Like Brett, any of us who have invested years in building a dream, only to see it wither and die, would be vastly disappointed. The majority of people want someone to listen to their dilemma, but they are not willing to change their lives. Sometimes you have to let part of you die to bring life to new dreams. Finding your way from Point A to Point B isn't always a straight or easy course. Sometimes your path zigzags in unforeseen ways. People might look at Brett's situation and say he failed. But if you experience burnout, it's a good indication that you need a new direction. It is okay to retreat and regroup. That's not failure—it's courage. When someone says, "The path you are on is not fruitful," it's difficult to admit that something is not working. It's much easier to continue and hope for the best, but any decision made in fear is a wrong decision.

If you want to go on a life adventure, you have to be willing to sacrifice and allow change to cost you. Since Brett was honest enough to permit truth-telling relationships into his life, he was able to make the difficult decision that empowered him to die to one dream and then pick up another. He was shell-shocked for a season, but pulled through and is better off than before. He sold his business, and now lives in the Midwest with his family. He has begun a new life journey. The weight of responsibility is gone, and he has recaptured vision for his life.

Assessment is what allowed me to stop and ask the difficult questions in my life when my little Lexie was born. It's not every day that a blue-eyed baby girl walks into your life and disturbs your heart rhythm. Her unexpected problems pulled me into a labyrinth of confusion, and I needed truth-tellers to help point the way to the next trail marker. How little I knew of what would come! After I pulled myself together from depression, a whole new life awaited me. There are no "rehearsals" on earth. This is our one chance to live life to the fullest. Wouldn't you be open to assessment if you knew it would help you live in the best possible way?

PERSONAL LEGEND

I believe there are two types of people: risk-takers and safe-players. Few have reached a balance between the two, but those who have, have unveiled a secret. They have found what I call their "Magnetic North." You might ask, "What do you mean by 'Magnetic North'?"

The earth's magnetic poles are not fixed, but continuously move due to disturbances in the geomagnetic field. Thus, when ancient explorers followed their compass according to a needle that always pointed north, they unknowingly navigated toward the magnetic north, not true north. So often when we embark on a life journey we see a fixed point before us, but struggle to reach it. This is because we have not factored in our uniqueness, or had an accurate reading of ourselves. Every person's Magnetic North is particular and cannot fit into someone else's mould. As we grow, develop and emerge into our true identity, our "fixed point" changes.

Our magnetic north is a compilation of the direction, goals, and dreams we believe we are heading toward. But sometimes, the point we are sailing toward changes over the course of our lives. Thus, we are led to our Magnetic North, a place where our gifts, talents and abilities align perfectly. When we reach Magnetic North, we might feel, *This is my destiny!* Although there was much to be gleaned from my days in the corporate world, during my time at the Wild at Heart conference, I was being set up for my Magnetic North. I would walk into the darkest moments of other's lives and help guide them into the light.

Magnetic North is what Paolo Coelho, the author of a brilliant yet simple fable, *The Alchemist*, calls our "Personal Legend." It's what we were born to do. Most of us remember that as children, we dreamed impossible dreams. The memories may be a bit dusty, but once we take them off the shelf and shake off the dust, we remember. For some, it was becoming an astronaut; for others, it might have been a fireman, a singer or dancer, a president or CEO of a major company, an athlete, or a number of other professions. As *The Alchemist* reads, "But, as time passes, a mysterious force begins to convince them that it will be impossible for them to realize their Personal Legend." [34] Many of us become discouraged along our life journey, and we either run too recklessly and burn out (the risk-takers), or we lose faith and live lives of "quiet desperation," feeling unfulfilled (the safe-players). [35]

MOVING PAST SAFE PLAYING

Not long ago I traveled to France to see my daughter, Amber. She and her husband Eric were traversing Europe experiencing and living life to the fullest. Amber takes after me in the sense that she is a task-oriented entrepreneur, and doesn't easily express emotion. Once upon a time, when Amber was an Indian Princess, we were close. But Lexie's death had taken its toll on everyone in our family, and somehow, Amber and I had lost our connection. Our conversations were superficial, rather than deep, like they used to be.

I had never taken Amber hiking before. Hiking had been something I did with the boys and for my own adventures with God. I went to France because I wanted an opportunity to connect with her on a deeper level, and I decided, "What better place that the backwoods of Europe?" If you have traveled to France, you know that the countryside, mountains and fertile valleys are inspiring! Just north of Cannes and Nice, there is a magnificent gorge named "Gorges du Verdon" in French, which means the "Canyon of Verdon."

As we journeyed along, the trail suddenly disappeared into a dark tunnel. "Did you bring a flashlight?" I asked Amber hopefully.

"Ah, nope!" she replied in her usual witty nature. Her body language told me she wasn't about to attempt the tunnel without one. "Actually, Dad," she continued, "The website did say something about flashlights..."

I thought of an idea. I reached into my backpack and rummaged around, looking for my iPhone. As soon as I pulled it out, Amber began to laugh.

"Wait! It's an application called 'flashlight'! Come on, Amber, pull yours out as well."

She didn't like my idea. "What if our batteries run out?"

I chuckled in response. That was a good question, but I knew we needed to take the risk anyway. "We'll be fine. Come on."

She trusted that she could follow me as I led the way into risk.

We stumbled and laughed as we nearly tiptoed through. The floor of the tunnel was wet and the sides were slimy. Soon, we found out that there were two more tunnels. *Will we have enough battery power for the return trip?* I questioned, but did not voice my thoughts to Amber. On several occasions, she hung on to my backpack. She was relying on my strength. Often, when you step outside your comfort zone into the unknown, it's like walking into a tunnel. The light behind you will guide you for a while, but soon it becomes so dark that you can't see what's ahead. You are completely sur-rounded by darkness. But if you keep walking forward, the light on the other side filters through. The farther you go, the brighter the light becomes.

After three tunnels, we came to the *real* test of resilience—a cliff. Outside the third tunnel, the trail curved upwards and narrowed along a granite cliff. In order to continue, we would have to go "hand over hand" and cling to the ropes. Needless to say, if we made one mistake, we could fall...to our deaths. I didn't want us to give up. I wanted us to conquer the seemingly unconquerable task.

But, Amber did not feel the same. "No way! Forget it, Dad." I noticed that her whole body was tense and she was anxious. Since her bus accident, she had never been able to face a circumstance that was "uncontrolled." She was not able to take risk like she had when she was younger, and had been playing it safe. This lack of risk had influenced her life decisions. I knew that if I let her have her way, she would continue to live in safety. Any circumstance that frightened her would control her by causing fear and convincing her to escape. I wanted to *guide* her to the truth. If she trusted me, I could help her be a victor.

"Amber," I began, looking into her eyes. "I would never put you

in a situation you can't handle. I know you can do this. I'll go first..."
Her eyes spoke of her fear, but also that she desired to trust me.
Then, I climbed up onto the granite slab and began inching along
the cliff, while holding onto the ropes. I made it across and looked
back at her. She was nervous. I knew it was a crossroad for her.
Would she trust her father? "You can do this, Amber," I coached. "I
will not let you fall."

As she took her first step to the granite slab, I knew she'd be fine.
She grabbed the ropes and began to move "hand over hand," "foot
over foot" across the cliff edge.

"You're doing great!" I called.

She made it across, and I could feel her confidence rise. On our
return, our iPhones granted us enough light to make it through
each tunnel. We continued to laugh about our crazy adventure.
However, I knew that the day hadn't been about adventure. She had
been limited by traumatic experiences and become a safe-player, yet
when she allowed me to gently nudge her in the right direction, she
was able to trust. She wasn't fighting for survival alone. She was a
beloved daughter. Amber and I had reconnected on a deep, spiritual
level. Through relationship, she conquered fear.

QUESTIONS FOR REFLECTION

1. Are you living a life that is based on fear? If so, what is it costing you?

2. How open are you to receiving feedback from an employee, etc.? Are you able to recognize if you "shut down" when given feedback?

CHAPTER 21

— Safe-players and Risk-takers —

"A ship in harbor is safe—
but that is not what ships are for."
JOHN A. SHEDD [36]

O NE OF MY favorite movies is *City Slickers*. The main character is a safe-player named Mitch Robbins (played by Billy
Crystal). Mitch has spent his career playing it "safe" in the corporate
world, hoping that it would eventually pay off. The movie is about
his vacation from regular life—a life that hasn't been working out
so well for him. Mitch is depressed, and burnt out with his business
and married life. He's never taken the risks he had always hoped he
would. Attempting to find some sense of meaning in the "wild," he
and his friends decide to herd cattle in the old fashioned way of the
American West.

The hard-riding boss of the trail is called Curly (played by Jack
Palance). He and Mitch have a conversation that illustrates the
mindset of many "safe-players":

> "Ah. There's nothing like bringing in a herd,"
> Curly sighed in satisfaction.

"Now see," Mitch began. "That's great. Your life makes sense to you."

Curly snickered.

"What's so funny?" Mitch protested.

"You city folks worry about a lot of shit."

"*Shit?* My wife basically told me she doesn't want me around!"

Curly continued to laugh and asked Mitch, "Is she a redhead?"

"I'm just saying…" Mitch defended himself, but Curly interrupted him.

"How old are you? Thirty-eight?"

"Thirty-nine."

"Yeah," Curly nodded his head. "You all come up here about the same age, the same problems. You spend fifteen years getting knots in your rope and then you think two weeks up here will untie them for you. None of you get it."

Silence.

Curly continued, "You know what the secret of life is?"

"No, I don't." Mitch protested.

Curly lifted his index finger. "This."

"Your finger?"

"One thing. Just *one* thing. You stick to that and everything else don't mean shit."

"That's great," Mitch said nonchalantly, not understanding Curly's intention. "But what's that 'one thing'?"

"That's what you have to figure out." Curly smiled in satisfaction. [37]

Obviously, Mitch's "one thing" wasn't a corporate life. He had never fulfilled his "wild side," and hoped that a week in the mountains would cure the symptoms. Many capable men, like Mitch, build their lives on safety, consistency and routine simply because taking a risk or making a change feels hazardous. Inevitably they end up basing life decisions on self-preservation. This keeps them in a day-to-day mode, where their energy is spent surviving rather than thriving in their God-given potential.

My bear story in Glacier National Park was no less of an accomplishment for me than Amber's risk climbing across the cliff, or Mitch's attempt to find that "one thing." I had become a safe-player after Lexie's death, caught in my own world of loss. But just as I had previously been required to step out of my comfort at Level 3, and trust God to take care of me and my family, so we are asked to leave safety behind and trust our Father. Many of us settle too much in life. We settle in our relationships, in our job, and sometimes even in our marriages. I fear that too many of us settle for less because we are afraid that we will fail in our attempt for the *more*. We make the best of our circumstances, but what if we were to ask God for more?

RISK-TAKERS

On the opposite extreme from safe-players are the risk-takers. They are thrilled by adventure, so much so that they are sometimes foolish. They are adrenaline-seekers and step out into risk without proper guidance or preparation. Yes, they may take a risk with a ten percent chance of victory and actually succeed. However, more often than not, they will keep propelling themselves in the same direction, regardless of the consequences. The risk may provide a thrilling experience at first, but inevitably, it can lead to burnout, business failure and fractured relationships. Worse yet, it can lead to life-threatening situations. In the story I am about to tell, three men plunged ahead in ignorant idealism, and suffered an irreparable tragedy.

During the bleak winter month of December in 2008, Kelly James, Brian Hall and Jerry Cooke attempted to climb Mount Hood, an 11,237-foot summit. They were die-hard risk-takers and obviously believed they were invincible. Their boldness was commendable, their idealism, infectious. They were able to push themselves to the limit of their ability. Their plan was to ascend the north face and then descend on the southern face. The climb included 2,000 feet of sheer ice where they would have to use ice picks and ropes. For experienced climbers, it took an average of twelve to fourteen hours. However, these three men did not have adequate experience. Plus, it was a harsh winter and daylight was shorter.

Experienced climbers are aware of risk and take precautions such as giving themselves more than enough hours to complete the task in case of emergency, keeping a steady pace, and starting out only a few hours after midnight. The trio began their climb from their overnight cabin at 6,000 feet well after the light of day, and their pace was far too slow. By mid-afternoon they were still ascending while heavy storm clouds gathered above their heads. Rather than turn back in safety, they decided to leave most of their gear behind and race to the summit. Without gear, with rain-soaked clothes and dropping temperatures, hypothermia set in. Once they reached the top, they could not turn around because the ice-slick slope was extremely hazardous. Attempting to get out of the storm, they dropped down the eastern side of the mountain. There they dug snow caves and waited, but the storm lasted for days and days. Rescuers could not get anywhere near them. Eventually the storm calmed, but another hit and a series of storms continued.

Kelly James was still alive on the afternoon of December 10 when he made a delusional call to his wife from his cell phone. "Hall went for help," he said. "Cooke is already safe on a plane." But neither Brian Hall nor Jerry Cooke were ever seen or heard from again. Kelly James' body was found a month later when a rescue crew was finally able to reach the supposed location of their death. [38]

These men failed to heed the warning signs before they hit a landslide. Their vision was grand, but they ran forward into risk without proper preparation. We cannot afford to take risks in life that could kill us, however attractive they seem.

REAGAN'S LEGACY

Then, there are those who lie somewhere in between risk-takers and safe-players. They have found a middle ground. They have settled into their Magnetic North. Ronald Reagan, President of the United States from 1981 to 1989, is one such man.

On March 30, 1981, Reagan's life was threatened. It was only seventy days after his inauguration. From the sidewalk near the Washington Hilton Hotel, John Hinckley Jr., fired six shots at the President. Reagan's Secret Service agents pushed him inside the limousine and rushed to a nearby hospital. Thankfully his life was spared and he became the first president in U.S. History to survive an assassination attempt while in office. This near-death experience was vital in propelling Reagan toward a life change. He entered a time of self-reflection that ultimately led him to his Magnetic North. It was obvious to many that his life had been spared for a reason. There was a grander purpose than even he had known. Mother Teresa said to him,

> You have suffered the passion of the cross and received grace. There is a purpose to this. Because of your suffering and pain, you will now understand the suffering and pain of this world. This has happened to you at this time because your country and the world need you. [39]

"Whatever happens now," Reagan wrote in his journal, "I owe my life to God and will try to serve Him in every way I can." [40]

During his two terms of office, Reagan passed an Economic Recovery Bill that enabled the United States to prosper, and reestablished relations with the Soviet Union—two seemingly unconquerable tasks. The Cold War between the Soviet Union and the United States had haunted their interactions for nearly a century, and was the major force in world politics. Mistrust and different government belief systems caused such a rift that there was almost always an unsaid threat of military war. Reagan was able to cultivate what was described as a "warm" relationship with Mikhail Gorbachev, general secretary of the Communist Party of the Soviet Union from 1985 to 1991, and dramatically decreased tension between the two world powers. [41] The British Prime Minister at the time, Margaret Thatcher, said of him, "Reagan ended the cold war without firing one shot." [42]

Part of the Cold War's brutal legacy was the Berlin Wall, an impenetrable concrete wall surrounded by mesh fencing and topped with barbed wire. It was built in 1961 by the German Democratic Republic in order to stop East Berliners from escaping the Soviet-controlled East German state to the West of the city, which was then occupied by the Americans, British and French. Over three hundred watchtowers glowered down on the "death strip," a one hundred yard area of land that separated the East from the West. If caught in an attempted escape, people were shot dead on sight. One hundred people were said to have died doing so, but their deaths did not hinder over 5,000 people escaping to freedom. [43] In June of 1987, Reagan stood in front of the graffiti-filled Berlin Wall and said, "Mr. Gorbachev, tear down this wall!" [44] Two years later East Germany was forced to open passage and its people began to tear the wall apart. The Cold War was over and the Soviet Union dissolved.

All of this occurred because after nearly losing his life, Reagan made a decision. He realigned himself to live out his full potential. This potential led to such prominent world events that his name will always be remembered in history. When we find our Magnetic North, as Reagan did, it is almost impossible for our lives to remain anonymous. The world cooperates with us. It is just as hungry for what we can give as we are to reach our convergence of gifting, talent and ability. As Coelho says, "When a person really desires something, all the universe conspires to help that person realize his dream." [45]

QUESTIONS FOR REFLECTION

1. Are you a risk-taker or a safe-player? How might you find a happy medium?

2. For what cause or for whom would you give your life? Why?

CHAPTER 22

—"I Want To Congratulate You"—

"History does not long entrust the care
of freedom to the weak or the timid."
DWIGHT D. EISENHOWER [46]

IN 2004, I attended a business conference. Its purpose was to create community and inspiration between entrepreneurs. At dinner one night, an unlikely woman complimented me. "I want to congratulate you on the life you have built, Mike," she said.

I assumed the woman was a trophy wife of another executive. I was wrong. She wasn't just another wife hanging on to the arm of her wealthy husband. She knew something about the corporate world, and I could tell that she could see past my exterior into the motivations of my heart, motivations that had transformed dramatically over the course of my life. Her words alluded to the fact that I had changed from a self-absorbed man, much like the man she was married to, into a man who knows that despite my success there is more to life than achievement.

I was humbled. I couldn't have received a more insightful compliment. After I walked back to my hotel room that night, I thought about what I wished I would have said in response (and maybe even directly to her husband), "Success, wealth and power are merely a shadow of a much larger plan."

Some of us believe that pursuing the American Dream will lead us to this larger plan, and it is thought to be a noble goal. This is what James Truslow Adams assumed when he coined the phrase, "The American Dream." His definition is as follows:

> It is not a dream of motor cars and high wages
> merely, but a dream of social order in which each
> man and each woman shall be able to attain to the
> fullest stature of which they are innately capable,
> and be recognized by others for what they are,
> regardless of the fortuitous circumstances of birth
> or position. [47]

This idyllic picture is noble, but it should be extended. Whether or not our goals are noble, we cannot simply remain self-interested. We must look deeper into the meaning of why we are alive and to what purpose we can serve. If we are not leaving something behind, we will inevitably feel empty. As I look back on that night, this is what I failed to explain to the woman who had complimented me.

WHAT IS PROSPERITY?

F. Scott Fitzgerald's cult classic, *The Great Gatsby*, published just a few years before Adam coined the phrase, explores the idea of the American Dream and its frailty. Jay Gatsby, one of the book's main characters, pursues "having it all" because he believes that if he simply works hard enough, he will achieve wealth and reach the pinnacle of society. The American Dream is attractive and desirable to him, like his love interest in the story, but it is also empty, and contentment eludes him. [48]

Like many of us at one point or another in our lives, Jay failed to realize that there is a difference between money, wealth and prosperity. Money is the accumulation of capital, which in itself, is shallow. There are benefits to having cash in the bank, but it's not intended exclusively for individual consumption. Money is amoral. If it's in the wrong hands, situations become ugly. It is a valuable tool *if* handled with purpose and right motive.

Wealth allows us to be financially independent (plus many other perks), but prosperity is true riches. Not only is it monetary gain, but it also includes purpose. So, how do we find our moral obligation for the money we have been given? Perhaps we should ask, "What did my parents model for me regarding money?" Most likely, our ideals about money stem from what we learned as children around the dinner table. As you know, my parents were honest citizens who worked and lived modestly. After years of pursuing monetary wealth, I stood by my father's deathbed, and suddenly knew (although it was never stated) that he believed he was the richest man alive because of *family*. He and my mother had raised eight children who were all happily married and productive members of society. To him, this was success. *This* was prosperity.

I believe that we are prosperous when we live beyond ourselves. Prosperity encapsulates all areas of life: from our finances to our marriage; our children; the ability to *choose* our path; and the freedom from spending our life as a workhorse for someone else's dream. When we live in a prosperous way, it attracts favor. Favor allows us to have a positive impact on our entire social network, which may include a city's poor or a nation's heads of state.

> Let not mercy and truth forsake you;
> Bind them around your neck,
> Write them on the tablet of your heart,
> *And* so find favor and high esteem
> In the sight of God and man. [49]

Prosperity also brings peace because our inherent disposition was designed to serve a greater purpose. Once we dedicate our lives to that purpose, the insatiable *more* that has haunted our soul is finally extinguished. John F. Kennedy rephrased the commission of Luke 12:48 and added his own memorable thoughts during a speech to the State House in Boston on January 9, 1961:

> For of those to whom much is given, much is required. And when at some future date the high court of history sits in judgment on each one of us—recording whether in our brief span of service we fulfilled our responsibilities to the state—our success or failure, in whatever office we may hold, will be measured by the answers to four questions.
>
> First, were we truly men of courage—with the courage…to resist public pressure, as well as private greed? Secondly, were we truly men of judgment—with…enough wisdom to know that we did not know, and enough candor to admit it?

Third, were we truly men of integrity—men...
whom neither financial gain nor political ambition
could ever divert from the fulfillment of our sacred
trust? Finally, were we truly men of dedication—
with an honor mortgaged to no single individual
or group, and compromised by no private obligation or aim, but devoted solely to serving the
public good and the national interest? [50]

In the same way, are we willing to ask ourselves, "To what purpose
have I been given prosperity?" My shift from egocentricity to prosperity, as you know, started with the trip to Sierra Leone, and began
to develop further during Lexie's lifetime. I'll never forget the look
on Robbie's face the day I said something that would have been
completely unorthodox just a few years before, "I just bought a
building!"

Robbie laughed and looked at Ty Schenzel, the man to whom
I was donating the building, and said, "Ty! What have you done to
my husband?"

"TO THE ONE WHO LIVES IN HOPELESSNESS..."

Remember, I had been the man who jabbed at another executive
at Taco Bell, "Why are you giving your time away? You are hurting
your chances of becoming financially successful!" Non-profit and
other such organizations were a waste of valuable time. But I had
changed. Now I finally understood the executive's motivation, and
it *felt* good.

I couldn't help but be drawn to Ty's passion to change the everyday lives of Omaha's inner-city youth. During Lexie's three years

of life, he had become a younger brother to me. He and his wife Terri stood by us faithfully in prayer and their strength added to our continually weakened state. You have to understand that a wealthy man has many friends, but for a wealthy man to find friends who ask nothing from him is rare. That's why it is so rewarding for me to be able to invest in others' lives when they haven't asked for it.

Ty didn't want anything from us. His mission was to be in relationship with the people I had misunderstood for much of my life. His labor was not easy. They worked out of a very small apartment in the worst, drug-infested and gang-filled areas of the city, providing school and weekend programs, hot meals, fun and games. I remember listening to countless stories of his interactions with people. When he had first begun, he was puzzled by the unending cycle of dysfunction, and continually sought out an answer to the question, "*Why* is there so much crime, shootings, homicides, dropping out of school, teen pregnancies, gang activity, and economic depression in this part of town?" He never found an answer until he heard a woman who was running for mayor, propose a life-changing thought during an address: "If you want to understand a lot of kids in my community, let me give you a phrase, 'To the one who lives in hopelessness, consequences mean nothing.'" Hopelessness had convinced the youth that, "Nothing's gonna change, so it's no use trying...." It was then that he realized the most significant goal beyond meeting the youth's physical needs—hope.

Each time he shared a new story, I felt something inside me say, *Maybe I can help....* That was daunting for a guy who had never paid attention to growing anyone or anything but himself. When I thought about what I (a wealthy executive without any practical experience that could help the "poor and needy") could do, I realized that Ty had time, but no money. His ministry survived off the benevolence of others. I had money, but no time. It was a perfect fit. If I could present him with enough money to create a self-sustaining program, his inner city "family" would experience prosperity.

One day, a business friend, Rik, Ty and myself drove to "New Jack City" as we fondly called the gang territory. Ty wanted to buy a larger and inexpensive building so that the numerous kids would have a place to hang out on the weekends. He was optimistic, but I was not impressed with the building. The roof had collapsed, the plumbing didn't work, and the floors and interior walls needed to be replaced.

"Ty," I said, realizing in that moment what it was I had to offer him. He was a pastor who loved disadvantaged kids. I had the business knowledge to help make him financially successful. "The building doesn't have investment potential. They should *give* it to you." Just as I needed Ty's skills in love without compensation, Ty needed my skills for how to set up an organization.

Then Rik added, "Are there other properties available in the neighborhood?"

Ty hesitated. "Well...there is a former Boys and Girls Club building, but it is huge."

"Let's go see it," I suggested.

As we toured the Boys and Girl's Club building, I knew it would be perfect. It was thirty thousand square feet, equipped with a gymnasium, an indoor swimming pool, a running track, a kitchen and classrooms. The Club had moved to a better facility in a different location and was looking for a buyer. All it needed was a little cleaning, and a few repairs, and Ty could run an incredible program!

"Okay, Ty," I said, barely able to contain my excitement. "Here's what we are going to do. Rik and I will buy the building and lease it to you for three years. If, after three years, you have made the ministry viable, meaning that you can demonstrate that the youth's lives are being changed for the better, that you can raise money, and make the ministry profitable, we will give you the building."

Ty's eyes filled with tears. I was handing him his dream.

"And of course," I joked, but meant every word, "We'll help you along the way."

We had a lot of work to do. Rik and I didn't want our investment to be part of a "well-intentioned" money vacuum. We'd walk alongside Ty's passion to help him set up performance criteria, a board of directors, enroll city and state leaders, and secure funding sources. Our goal was to ensure that the youth had a healthy and safe place to receive tutoring, an evening meal, learn how to be better athletes, have fun, and to hear about God if they chose.

In lieu of Ty's vision for hope, we called the new building the "Hope Center." When its doors opened the first day, one hundred youth, ranging in age from seven to nineteen, gathered around its doors, ready to receive everything we had to give. We charged five dollars per year and asked for parents or guardians to volunteer. Eventually, thirty-two local churches became part of our support team. Due to Ty's enthusiasm, and my connections in the corporate world, we convinced some of the most important business leaders in the state to lend their support. The mayor of Omaha visited several times, and often brought U.S. senators or congressmen.

To whoever would listen, Ty would say,

> You can live without food for forty days. You can
> live without water for a week. None of us can live

long without hope. When you don't have hope,
like many of these kids, you can be thrown in jail
or die on the streets. It doesn't matter. Consequences mean nothing. Without hope, you don't
have anything.

Because of Ty's passion, the Hope Center has been a success!
Through the support of their programs, ninety percent graduate
from high school and sixty percent go on to college. These statistics
are in stark contrast to nearly all socio-economically depressed areas
in the United States.

QUESTIONS FOR REFLECTION

1. How would you define prosperity?

2. What are ways in which your life displays it?

CHAPTER 23

Ending Well

"Our remedies oft in ourselves do lie,
Which we ascribe to heaven."
WILLIAM SHAKESPEARE [51]

Nᴏᴛ ʟᴏɴɢ after losing Lexie, Robbie and I moved our family to Santa Barbara, California. By that time, I had begun several exploits following my personal legend as a "guide." What began as simply helping people with business ideas, and offering career and financial advice, grew into serving as a board member for non-profit and for-profit entities, like Habitat for Humanity; and leadership training for churches, including the International House of Prayer in Kansas City. However, nothing seemed to prepare me more than the Santa Barbara Rescue Mission.

The Rescue Mission was a faith-based facility that coached men and women out of their addictions by finding the root of pain. Not only did they receive inner healing, but the Mission helped them through their legal issues, provided a way for them to finish their education and find long-term, sustainable jobs. Due to the Mission's skill and rigorous program, it had one of the highest success rates of people staying "clean" after graduation.

Just a few years before, I had associated with the highly educated, business executives, and those who had every monetary advantage in life at their disposal. At the Mission, I was a mentor to the "poor and needy"—the people I used to avoid. Many of those at the Mission had a criminal record, suffered abuse, and had at one point been homeless. Because of Lexie, I was now living in a different world. I even overheard a woman at my church state, "My pastor is Mike Frank."

I nearly fell off my chair. *Me? Pastoral?* What I hadn't realized was that I was not just becoming a man who was courageous enough to stare difficultly in the eye, but also a *father* to others. *Wow! I must have had some major heart surgery!*

When I began coaching the Executive Director, I also became friends with a man named Joe. [52] As a child, Joe's dad would quote Bible verses as he lashed him with his belt. He grew up in a world of contradiction, and later suffered from several addictions to try and numb the pain. When he was old enough, he escaped home by joining the Navy. But, when he returned to California several years later, his choices caused him to become an alcoholic and drug user. Eventually, he had nothing left and was living in a cardboard box on Skid Row in Los Angeles. In that untouchable realm of the city, he was finally arrested and sent to the Rescue Mission in Santa Barbara.

Not long after building a relationship with those at The Mission, the Executive Director decided to step down and the board asked me to take his place as the interim Director.

"You're kidding!" I quipped jokingly to them. *Have I changed that much?* I asked myself.

The board members' faces were serious, yet they couldn't hold back their smiles. "No, Mike. We're not kidding."

Is this really a part of Your plan, God? I was shocked, but I knew it was right. Robbie and I both became more involved, and the love I developed for the people surprised me. I was able to walk alongside Joe. He finished high school, studied to receive an Associate's Degree in Counseling, and found a wife. He soon became the Director of Men's Programs and I taught him how to speak in public so that he became our primary spokesperson. Often, I would gaze at the men and woman and remember Lexie. Then I would hear God say to me, *That is how I see you, Mike. You are broken, but I love you anyway.*

TOM HILL'S CORE PRINCIPLES

With blue eyes that glow and a crown of silver hair, Tom Hill carries a fatherly and affirming presence. Everyone loves him. He compliments others in such a way that they feel safe with him. Before they realize it, they have opened their hearts. People are at their best after spending time with him. His life goal is to help others be the best they can be. He even carries a $100.00 bill in his pocket to give away at any given moment.

After spending twenty-six years as a professor and administrator for the University of Missouri, Tom decided to pursue a career in real estate franchise sales. Ten years later his company grossed over three billion. Essentially, he has acquired the American Dream, but he has also challenged himself to look beyond his success. He is well known and respected by top executives in the United States, and because of this, he has often been a speaker for executive leadership organizations.

During a session at a business summit, he said, "I have built my life on three core principles."

I listened intently, hoping to glean words of wisdom from a man who has built a legacy.

"First, I believe people have the moral obligation to be the very best they can be."

Check, I thought. *I agree with that one. It's a shame when someone has potential but chooses to waste it.*

"Second," Tom continued, "People have the moral obligation to make a positive difference with every person they meet. Whether it is someone in your family, a cab driver, flight attendant, or your boss, I challenge you to ask, 'What can I do to enhance this person's life?'"

True. He's speaking my language. That's what life is all about. Tom wasn't just stating philosophic principles. He lived them. I had often seen him walk up to a complete stranger to say something encouraging. He cultivated a gift of believing in people, and it has taken him beyond the ordinary definition of success into the *more* of leaving a legacy.

"Finally," Tom concluded, "You can never dream big enough." He went on to describe a life-changing event that occurred by listening to one of the world's top inspirational speakers, Jim Rohn.

Jim asked his listeners, "How tall can a tree grow?"

Tom had no idea.

Then Jim said, "As tall as it can."

In that moment, Tom's wife Betty looked at him and stated, "Honey, you haven't grown as tall as you can."

Wow, I thought. *To reach our full potential, we must live all three core principals: aiming to be our best, serving others, and not letting anything hinder our growth.* Only then will we grow as high as possible.

ENDING WELL

To end well means to live our lives with relentless purpose. It means our days are adventurous, not obligatory or something to be feared. Often, life doesn't lead us in the way we imagine. We won't know what is inside the dark tunnel, or even on the other side. "*It is* the glory of God to conceal a matter, but the glory of kings *is* to search out a matter." [53] For some of us, "searching out the matter" includes tragedy and sorrow. For others, it may have unforeseen twists and turns, but if we are able to push forward into the resistance, we will come out stronger on the other end. We must trust that our Father will protect us, even if we don't understand the circumstances.

There are many things I did not do correctly along my journey. But, there are also many things for which I am thankful. Where would I be if Amber's near death had not propelled me toward God; if Dustin's personality hadn't required me to look past my left-brained ideals; if Robbie hadn't challenged me to live out her dreams; if Christian hadn't brought me joy during the darkest season of my life, and if Lexie hadn't been born? I would be a "poser," a man who doesn't know his true identity. I would be a man whose heart is cold toward others. I would still be chasing after an empty explanation of success.

I was willing, although regretfully at times, to examine my life and sometimes make difficult decisions. I ask you to do the same, "Are you really willing to examine your life and ask the tough questions?" My journey toward success was, in a sense, hijacked by life's demands. But I am ever so thankful. I was broken apart by love for my little girl, Lexie, whom I'm anxious to meet again someday.

Now I would define success differently. Success isn't power, money, influence or prestige. In the last few years, I have sat down to evaluate my life, and thought...

I am no longer the narrow-focused high flyer who is far removed from outside trauma, unable to come close enough to suffering to feel its unjust stench. The anxiety about my own progression and vitality is gone. I have experienced suffering firsthand, and have come to understand how my talents and connections benefit others. I have begun a journey that is fundamental to any man, whether business executive or priest—to be trusted with the hearts of others.

I am not afraid to state that I'm still growing. I am a man on a journey. But recognizing the journey's purpose has brought me peace, and I'm gaining confidence as I stare at the long road ahead. In the distance, the light wavers, blurring the road's direction. I cannot see its end, but I anticipate an unspeakable horizon. With assurance I can share that I've acted as guide for many lives, and the fulfillment it's brought me is beyond comprehension. I am continually pursuing the *more,* although I feel content, much like my father did about our family.

If you have recognized it or not, your life is rife with prosperity— either in relationship, family, career, finances or faith. Understanding your prosperity is the beginning of the journey, but let us go further. My final challenge to you is, "How will you bring *purpose* to your prosperity?"

ACKNOWLEDGEMENTS

This book would not have been possible without the help from many people. It would be impossible to name everyone. However, I would like to single out a few.

Thank you to my wife Robbie. I can't believe God gave you to me, even after thirty-four years of marriage. You've been my lover, my partner, and I can't imagine the journey without you. I would also like to thank my daughter Amber, and my sons Dustin and Christian. You've allowed me to father you and have brought such joy into our lives.

Eileen Chambers, thank you for helping to draw out and select the important stories we share within the book.

A special thanks to Vanessa Chandler for using her God-given gifts to make this book possible. You believed in me and my story, constantly encouraged me, and asked great questions. I'd also like to thank Blair Reynolds for believing in the story and bringing insight and organization.

There have been so many people who have influenced my life in one way or another. By influencing me, you have shaped my life direction. You know who you are, and thank you to all of you.

Thank you, God, for providing the adventure and inviting me to participate.

ENDNOTES

1 Albert Einstein, quoted on *Refspace.com*, accessed June 20, 2011, http://refspace.com/quotes/LIFE.

2 Excerpt from *The Wizard Of Oz* Granted Courtesy Of Warner Bros. Entertainment Inc. All Rights Reserved ©1939.

3 Adam Smith, quoted on *Thinkexist.com*, accessed June 20, 2011, http://www.thinkexistcom.

4 David Kenyon Webster, quoted on *Thinkexist.com*, accessed June 21, 2011, http://thinkexist.com/quotations/sacrifice/2.html.

5 St. Thomas Aquinas, quoted on CreatingMinds.org, accessed June 16, 2011, http://creatingminds.org/quotes/self.htm.

6 Promise Keepers is a ministry geared to promote spiritual health and integrity in men. (See: http://www.promisekeepers.org/).

7 François de La Rochefoucauld, quoted on HeartQuotes Center, HeartMath LLC, accessed June 21, 2011, http://www.heartquotes.net/Heart-quotes.html.

8 Vanessa J. Chandler, quoted in person to author.

9 Henry David Thoreau, quoted on The Quote Garden, accessed August 3, 2011, http://www.quotegarden.com/self-discovery.html.

10 "MFS and UUNET Announce Merger Agreement to Form Premier Internet Business Communications Company," *Business Wire*, April 30, 1996, via The Free Library, www.thefreelibrary.com, accessed June 16, 2011.

11 Leonardo da Vinci, quoted on *BrainyQuote*, accessed June 21, 2011, http://www.brainyquote.com/quotes/keywords/honor.html.

12 Michael Desenne, "SMARTMONEY: A Grim Fairy Tale," *The Wall Street Journal*, December 31, 2002, accessed June 21, 2011, http://www.smartmoney.com/invest/stocks/a-grim-fairy-tale-13730/.

13 "Triumph of the Nerds," THE TELEVISION PROGRAM TRANSCRIPTS: PART III, *Pbs.org,* accessed June 17, 2011, http://www.pbs.org/nerds/part3.html.

14 C.S. Lewis, *The Problem of Pain,* (New York: HarperOne, 2001), 91. Copyright CS Lewis Pte Ltd.

15 Charles Caleb Colton, quoted on *BrainyQuote,* accessed June 21, 2011, http://www.brainyquote.com/quotes/keywords/shipwreck.html.

16 Winston Churchill, quoted on *The Quote Garden*, accessed June 21, 2011, http://www.quotegarden.com/adversity.html.

17 Warren Bass, "The Great Leveling," *The Washington Post*, Sunday, April 3, 2005; Page BW03

18 Ralph Waldo Emerson, "Memory," quoted on Notable Quotes, accessed June 21, 2011, http://www.notable-quotes.com/m/memory_quotes.html.

19 Theodore Roosevelt, quoted on *BrainyQuote*, accessed June 23, 2011, http://www.brainyquote.com/quotes/keywords/suffering.html.

20 Author Unknown, quoted in "Quotes and Sayings about Death," *The Quote Garden*, accessed June 23, 2011, http://www.quotegarden.com/death.html.

21 Horatio Gates Spafford, quoted in "A Hymn and its History," *Bible Study Charts*, accessed June 17, 2011, http://www.biblestudycharts.com/A_Daily_Hymn.html.

22 Johann Friedrich Von Schiller, quoted on *BellaOnline*, accessed July 8, 2011, http://www.bellaonline.com/articles/art40878.asp.

23 John Adams, quoted in "Our Presidents," *The White House*, accessed June 17, 2011, http://www.whitehouse.gov/about/presidents/johnadams.

24 John Adams, quoted on *The Quotations Page*, accessed June 17, 2011, www.thequotationspage.com.

25 John Eldredge, *Desire: The Journey We Must Take to Find the Life God Offers* (Nashville: Thomas Nelson, 2007), 12.

26 John Eldredge, *The Ransomed Heart: A Collection of Devotional Readings* (Nashville: Thomas Nelson, 2005), 175.

27 Ralph Waldo Emerson, quoted on *BrainyQuote*, accessed June 17, 2011, www.brainyquote.com.

28 William Blake, *The William Blake Archive*, Ed. Morris Eaves, Robert N. Essick, and Joseph Viscomi, accessed June 17, 2011, http://www.blakearchive.org.

29 Ibid.

30 Ibid.

31 Bill Johnson, pastor of *Bethel Church* in Redding, CA, http://www.ibethel.org.

32 Ralph Waldo Emerson, quoted on *The Adventure of Life*, accessed June 23, 2011, http://www.nsrider.com/quotes/life.htm.

33 Pythagoras, quoted on *Decision Innovation*, accessed June 23, 2011, http://www.decision-making-solutions.com/decision_making_quotes.html.

34 Paolo Coelho, *The Alchemist* (New York: HarperCollins, 1996), 22.

35 Henry David Thoreau, *Walden*, Chapter 1-A, accessed June 17, 2011, http://thoreau.eserver.org/walden1a.html.

36 John A. Shedd, *Salt from My Attic* (1928), quoted on The Quotations Page, accessed June 23, 2011, http://www.quotationspage.com/quote/34287.html.

37 Excerpt FROM CITY SLICKERS GRANTED COURTESY OF WARNER BROS. ENTERTAINMENT INC.

38 "Mount Hood Climbing Accidents," *Wikipedia.org*, accessed June 17, 2011, http://en.wikipedia.org/wiki/Mount_Hood_climbing_accidents. Oakley Brooks, "OUTDOORS; Challenging Mount Hood A Month After a Tragedy," *New York Times*, January 20, 2007, accessed June 17, 2011, http://query.nytimes.com/gst/fullpage.html?res=9405E5D91E30F933A15752C0A9619C8B63.

39 Mother Teresa, quoted by Dinesh D'Souza in *Ronald Reagan: How an Ordinary Man Became an Extraordinary Leader* (New York: Simon & Schuster, 1999), 207.

40 John O'Sullivan, *The President, the Pope, and the Prime Minister: Three Who Changed the World* , (Washington, D.C.: Regnery Publishing, Inc., 2006), 87.

41 "Cold War," *GlobalSecurity.org*, accessed June 17, 2011, http.//www.globalsecurity.org/military/ops/cold_war.htm.

42 Margaret Thatcher, quoted in "President Ronald Reagan: Winning the Cold War," *HISTORYNET.COM*, accessed July 6, 2011, http://www.historynet.com/president-ronald-reagan-winning-the-cold-war.htm.

43 "The Berlin Wall," *Berlin-life.com*, accessed June 17, 2011, http://www.berlin-life.com.

44 Ronald Reagan, quoted by Michael K. Deaver in *A Different Drummer, My Thirty Years with Ronald Reagan* (New York: HarperCollins, 2001), 176.

45 Coelho, *The Alchemist*, 121.

46 President Dwight D. Eisenhower's inaugural address, 20 January 1953, University of Iowa Libraries. Government Publications Dept., accessed June 23, 2011, http://digital.lib.uiowa.edu/cdm4/item_viewer.php?CISOROOT=/gpc&CISOPTR=621&CISOBOX=1&REC=7.

47 James Truslow Adams, *Epic of America* (Boston: Little Brown & Company, 1931), 214-215.

48 F. Scott Fitzgerald, *The Great Gatsby* (New York: Scribner, 1999).

49 Proverbs 3:3-4.

50 John F. Kennedy, "Speech," *The Official Website of the Commonwealth of Massachusetts*, The State House, Boston, January 9, 1961, accessed June 13, 2011, http://www.mass.gov/.

51 William Shakespeare, *All's Well that Ends Well*, 1.1.215-6, quoted in *The Riverside Shakespeare*, edited by G. Blakemore Evans (Houghton Mifflin Company, 1974), 507.

52 Name is fictitious to protect identity.

53 Proverbs 25:2.

FRANK
CONSULTING

Frank Consulting focuses on inspiring and encouraging entrepreneurs. Mike Frank is a recognized expert on taking leaders to higher levels of performance and impact, with more than three decades of senior-level executive experience at multi-national Fortune 500 corporations, start-up entrepreneurial ventures and non-profits.

for more information visit:
www.mikefrankconsulting.com

Slingstone Media is a relationally based publishing house. Each year, we select a limited number of societally transformative texts. Authors include experienced professionals with proven expertise in the realms of business, government, education, spiritual life and family. We aspire to create inspirational, innovative and artistic texts utilizing contemporary technology.

SLINGSTONE
M E D I A

www.slingstonemedia.com